SAINT

PATRICK

by
William J. Federer

© William J. Federer, 2002. All Rights Reserved.
No prior permission is necessary to reproduce 5000 words or less
provided acknowledgment given to: *Saint Patrick* by William J. Federer

Library of Congress

HISTORY / INSPIRATION   ISBN 0-9653557-5-6   UPC 82189800010
Cover photos: (front) *Saint Patrick*, Sonia Haliday Photographs, *Great Leaders of the Christian Church*,
Moody Press, Chicago, 1988; (back) *Saint Patrick Climbs Croagh Patrick* by Margaret Clarke/ Hugh Lane
Municipal Gallery of Modern Art, Dublin, Christian History, Carol Stream, Illinois, Issue 60.

Amerisearch, Inc., P.O. Box 20163, St. Louis, MO 63123, 1-888-USA-WORD
314-487-4395 voice/fax, www.amerisearch.net, wjfederer@aol.com

Table of Contents

FOREWORD

He was not a leprechaun, an elf, nor full of blarney. He did not drink green beer, wear a "Kiss me, I'm Irish" pin, or lead a parade in New York or Boston. He did not hide a pot of gold at the end of the rainbow, but what did do brought something more valuable than gold into the lives of thousands. His name was Patrick.

The Life of

Patrick

c. 389	Birth in Roman Britain.
405-411	Captivity as a slave in Ireland.
431	Palladius's mission to Ireland.
432	Patrick's mission to Ireland.
?461	Death in Ireland.

Armagh •

Ireland

Great Leaders of the Christian Church, John D. Woodbridge, Moody Press, Chicago

SAINT PATRICK

BIRTH

Patrick was born in the latter part of the 4th century possibly around A.D. 387,[1] but scholars differ, with some placing it as late as A.D. 415.[2] His home was in Bonavem Taberniae, (Roman Britain.) One possible location may have been the town of Alcluyd on the River Clyde. Alcluyd means "The Rock of Clyde, " which was a Roman stronghold, later called "Dumbarton." A site there, known as "Kilpatrick" is marked as his birthplace.[3] Other possible locations are: Caerwent, near Chepstow, Monmouthshire;[4] Tiburnia near Holyhead in western Wales;[5] or Glamorganshire, South Wales.[6]

Patrick died on March 17th at Downpatrick, Ireland. Scholars differ on the year, citing from A.D. 461[7] to A.D. 493.[8] Monasteries at Armagh, Downpatrick, and Saul claim his remains.[9]

Two writings of Patrick's have been validated by scholars as

Hadrian's Wall marked the northern frontier of the Roman Empire. Roman troops were withdrawn from Britain in A.D. 407, never to return.

unquestionably authentic: *The Confession of Patrick* and his *Letter to Coroticus.* The *Confession,* which contains approximately 200 references to scripture, includes *The Rule of Faith of the Trinity,* a creed of the ancient Church.

Patrick was raised in a respected Roman family, with his father, Calpurnius, being a civil magistrate, holding the office of *decurio,* and serving as a deacon in the church. His grandfather, Potitus, held a ministry position in the Church, whose origins date from the 2nd century Roman occupation of Britain.[10]

Patrick's mother, Conchessa, taught him to pray, but by his own admission, Patrick had not committed his life to God till he had been in captivity several years. In his *Confession* (translated from Latin by Ludwig Bieler), Patrick wrote:

> "I am Patrick, a sinner, most unlearned, the least of all the faithful, and utterly despised by many. My father was Calpornius, a deacon, son of Potitus, a priest, of the village Bannavem Taburniæ; he had a country seat nearby, and there I was taken captive. I was then about sixteen years of age. I did

Saint Patrick

not know the true God. I was taken into captivity to Ireland with many thousands of people – and deservedly so, because we turned away from God, and did not keep His commandments."[11]

"As a youth, nay, almost as a boy not able to speak, I was taken captive, before I knew what to pursue and what to avoid."[12]

THE WORLD

Patrick was born at a time when the great Roman Empire was decaying. Britain had seceded from Roman authority and briefly saw a resurgence of Celtic culture prior to the Germanic invasions in later centuries.

The Roman Empire, at whose power the world stood in awe, was now suffering irreparably with problems such as:

- Infidelity, lust, perversion, all of which had become commonplace. The 5th century writer, Salvian, wrote "The Goths lie, but are chaste, the Franks lie, but are generous, the Saxons are savage in cruelty ... but are admirable in chastity .... What hope can there be for the Romans when the barbarians are more pure than they?"[13]

- Roman bath houses and gymnasiums became places of immorality and homosexuality. ("gymn" is the Greek word for "naked."). Salvian wrote: "O Roman people be ashamed; be ashamed of your lives. Almost no cities are free of evil dens, are altogether free of impurities, except the cities in which the barbarians have begun to live....Let nobody think otherwise. The vices of our bad lives have alone conquered us."[14]

- Exposure of unwanted infants in pagan temples or outside city, allowing them to die; Christians would gather children, nurse to health, raise them, with many of them becoming great leaders.

- Violence in sports, gladiatorial events, entertainment, with people growing insensitive and callused, desiring personal gratification, "in the causal brutality of its public spectacles, in a rampant immorality that even Christianity could not check."[15]

- The value of human life was low. Slavery abounded, especially of the captured peoples from Eastern Europe known as "Slavs." "Slavs," which meant "glorious" came to have the inglorious meaning of "slave."[16]

- Abandoning of the city centers by the upper class to palatial suburban estates. The educated and skilled pursued business and financial success, to the neglect of their involvement in politics. Lead poisoning was also a problem in cities, as water was brought in through lead pipes. (The Latin word for lead is *plumb* or *plumbing*.)

- Injustice in legal system, favor given to those of financial means within the courts.

- Taxes became unbearable. "Collectors became greedy functionaries in a bureaucracy so huge and corrupt." Tax collectors were described by Salvian as "more terrible than the enemy."[17]

- Welfare and government jobs exploded. One Roman commented "Those who live at the expense of the public funds are more numerous than those who provide them."[18]

- Trade Deficit – "The Western Roman economy, already undermined by falling production of the great Roman estates and an unfavorable balance of trade that siphoned off gold to the East, had now run out of money."[19]

- Dependence of Foreign Trade – "As conquerors of North Africa, the Vandals cut off the Empire's grain supply at will. This created critical food shortages, which in turn curtailed Roman counterattacks."[20]

- Huge Bureaucratic Machinery was unable to govern the empire effectively with the enormous debt.

- Military was cut back to dangerously low ranks, over-extended boundaries, fighting on several fronts.

- "The church, while preaching against abuses, contributed to the decline by discouraging good Christians from holding public office."[21]

- The Roman Empire was being invaded by Germanic Tribes: Franks, Saxons, Vandals, Ostrogoths, Visigoths, Burgundians, Lombards, Anglos, Jutes. It was threatened by African Berbers, Picts of northern Britain, nomadic Arab raiders, Persians, Tribes, and the Huns, of which Attila was king. (The Huns attacked other tribes, such as the Visigoths, forcing them into Roman territory.) Rome was sacked for the first time in A.D. 410 by the Visigoths, A.D. 455 by the Vandals, A.D. 476 by the Ostrogoths, which is considered the official fall of Rome, and many more times before A.D. 563.

Patrick, as a boy on his father's farm near the sea shore.

People in History—From Caractacus to Alfred, R.J. Unstead, Carousel Books, Transworld Publishers Ltd, Great Britain

Irish raiders capture Patrick.

- The Latin Language was being displaced with the native languages of the foreign tribes crossing the borders.

TRAGEDY

Patrick's British name at birth was Sucat, but his Latin name was "Patricius," meaning "Noble." Around 405 A.D., at the age of 16 years old, while working of his father's farm near the sea, 50 *currachs* (longboats) filled with raiders weaved their way toward the shore. Mary Cagney, author of the article "Patrick The Saint" (Christian History, Issue 60), wrote:

"With no Roman army to protect them (Roman legions had long since deserted Britain to protect Rome from barbarian invasions), Patricius and his town were unprepared for attack. The Irish warriors, wearing helmets and armed with spears, descended on the pebble beach. The braying war horns struck terror into Patricius' heart, and he started to run toward town. The warriors quickly demolished the village, and as Patricius darted among the burning houses and screaming women, he was caught. The barbarians dragged him aboard a boat bound for the east coast of Ireland."[22]

In his *Confession,* Patrick wrote:

"And the Lord brought over us the wrath of his anger and scattered us among many nations, even unto the utmost part of the earth, where now my littleness is placed among strangers." [23]

Patrick was brought to Ireland, where he was sold as a slave to a cruel warrior chief named Milchu, who was the local Ulster chieftain, and possible druid high priest, who ruled in area of Dalriada or Antrim.[24]

Most likely, Patrick saw the heads of the conquered enemies impaled atop sharp poles around the palisade in Northern Ireland. There Patrick worked herding his masters pigs or sheep on the nearby hill, living like an animal, enduring long bouts of hunger and thirst.[25] For the next six years, this was Patrick's life.

TEENAGER

Lonely and sad among these strange, fierce people, Patrick saw their infatuation with superstition and magic spells. He became repulsed by their Druid priests who led the people in worship of the sun, moon, wind, water, fire, rocks, and even human sacrifice.

According to Thomas Cahill, author of *How the Irish Saved Civilization* (Doubleday, 1995), the Druids:

"sacrificed prisoners of war to the war gods and newborns to the harvest gods. Believing that the human head was the seat of the soul, the displayed proudly the heads of their enemies in their temples and on their palisades; they even hung them from their belts as ornaments, used them as footballs in victory celebrations, and were fond of employing skull tops as ceremonial drinking bowls. They also sculpted heads– both shrunken, decapitated heads."[26]

The Druids, from whom Halloween originated, believed that the trees and hills were inhabited by good and evil spirits which had to be appeased or they would bring harm. This worship of demons has come down to the present day in the guise "trick or treat" and elves and leprechauns.

In his crisis, Patrick turned to Christ. He remembered the faith of his father and grandfather, as well as the prayers of his mother. He wrote in his *Confession*:

Irish tree trunk

"But after I came to Ireland---every day I had to tend sheep, and many times a day I prayed---the love of God and His fear came to me more and more, and my faith was strengthened. And my spirit was moved so that in a single day I would say as many as a hundred prayers, and almost as many in the night, and this even when I was staying in the woods and on the mountains; and I used to get up for prayer before daylight, through snow, through frost, through rain, and I felt no harm, and there was no sloth in me---as I now see, because the spirit within me was then fervent."[27]

CONVERSION

While watching his master's herds, Patrick would kneel and pray on the grassy slopes of the valley of Braid and on the slopes of Slemish, near what is now the town of Ballymena.[28] He would pray to God to help him to be brave and good. It was during his years of captivity that he began to reflect on his spiritual condition, and truly committed himself to Christ. He wrote:

"And there the Lord opened the sense of my unbelief that I might at last remember my sins and be converted with all my heart to the Lord my God, who had regard for my abjection, and mercy on my youth and ignorance, and watched over me before I knew Him, and before I was able to distinguish between good and evil, and guarded me, and comforted me as would a father his son."[29]

ESCAPE

From this time on, Patrick's life became marked by times of intense and persistent prayer. He became conscious of an "inner monition" in response to his prayers, which he recognized as the voice of the Holy Spirit answering him. It was this that spoke to him to escape and make his way to the sea-coast

Patrick takes wolf-hounds aboard ship.

where he would find a ship to take him to freedom.

In his *Confession*, Patrick wrote:

> "And there one night I heard in my sleep a voice saying to me: `It is well that you fast, soon you will go to your own country.' And again, after a short while, I heard a voice saying to me: `See, your ship is ready.' And it was not near, but at a distance of perhaps two hundred miles, and I had never been there, nor did I know a living soul there; and then I took to flight, and I left the man with whom I had stayed for six years. And I went in the strength of God who directed my way to my good, and I feared nothing until I came to that ship." [30]

Patrick obeyed the inner voice of the Holy Spirit, escaped. He ran and hid for days, covering nearly 200 miles, till he at last came to the shore, probably Killala Bay or Westport. There he found the ship of which he was foretold, possibly carrying Irish wolfhounds to the European. [31]

He wrote in his *Confession*:

> "And the day that I arrived the ship was set afloat, and I said that I was able to pay for my passage with them. But the captain was not pleased, and

with indignation he answered harshly: `It is of no use for you to ask us to go along with us.' And when I heard this, I left them in order to return to the hut where I was staying. And as I went, I began to pray; and before I had ended my prayer, I heard one of them shouting behind me, `Come, hurry, we shall take you on in good faith; make friends with us in whatever way you like.' And so on that day I refused to suck their breasts for fear of God, but rather hoped they would come to the faith of Jesus Christ, because they were pagans. And thus I had my way with them, and we set sail at once." [32]

R.J. Unstead, in his book *People in History-From Caractacus to Alfred* (London, Transworld Publishers, Ltd., 1975), wrote:

> "He came upon some sailors who were leading a number of fierce-looking dogs toward the ship, which was drawn up on the shore.
> 'Sailor,' cried Patrick, 'where are you going, and when do you leave?'
> 'We sail in an hour' answered the tall seaman. 'We are bound for Britain, to sell these wolfhounds for hunting.'
> 'Can I go with you?' asked Patrick eagerly.
> 'If you can mind these dogs in a rough sea, you can come,' said the sailor, 'Here take this pair aboard.'
> Patrick joyfully agreed, and the men were astonished at the way the great dogs at once obeyed him." [33]

TESTING

As they left Ireland for Britain, a storm blew them off course to Gaul (France.) The region where they landed had been recently ravaged by war. "Goths or Vandals had so decimated the land that no food was to be found in the once fertile area." [34] They traveled for days without food and water. Patrick wrote in his *Confession*:

"And after three days we reached land, and for twenty-eight days we traveled through deserted country. And they lacked food, and hunger overcame them; and the next day the captain said to me: `Tell me, Christian: you say that your God is great and all-powerful; why, then, do you not pray for us? As you can see, we are suffering from hunger; it is unlikely indeed that we shall ever see a human being again.'

I said to them full of confidence: `Be truly converted with all your heart to the Lord my God, because nothing is impossible for Him, that this day He may send you food on your way until you be satisfied; for He has abundance everywhere.' And, with the help of God, so it came to pass: suddenly a herd of pigs appeared on the road before our eyes, and they killed many of them; and there they stopped for two nights and fully recovered their strength, and their hounds received their fill for many of them had grown weak and were half-dead along the way. "[35]

The party Patrick was with offered him food, but upon hearing they had previously offered it in sacrifice to their pagan gods, Patrick refused:

"And from that day they had plenty of food. They also found wild honey, and offered some of it to me, and one of them said: `This we offer in sacrifice.' Thanks be to God, I tasted none of it."[36]

Patrick recounted that on the same day they ran out of food, they providentially met people who would help them:

"Also on our way God gave us food and fire and dry weather every day, until, on the tenth day, we met people. As I said above, we traveled twenty-eight days through deserted country, and the night that we met people we had no food left."[37]

Patrick soon realized that the raiders began to consider him their captive. Facing the dim prospect of more enslavement, after his six years of slavery in Ireland, he wrote:

> "And once again, after many years, I fell into captivity. On that first night I stayed with them, I heard a divine message saying to me: 'Two months will you be with them.' And so it came to pass: on the sixtieth night thereafter the Lord delivered me out of their hands."[38]

YEARS IN EUROPE

Patrick did not elaborate in his *Confession* what happened in the intervening years before his return to Britain, except:

> "And again after a few years I was in Britain with my people, who received me as their son, and sincerely besought me that now at last, having suffered so many hardships, I should not leave them and go elsewhere."[39]

Evidence points to him spending time at St. Martin's monastery at Tours, and "many scholars believe Patrick spent a period training for ministry in Lerins, an island off the south of France near Cannes,"[40] possibly secluding himself in a monastery on the island of St. Honorat, off the coast of the French Riviera.[41]

THE CALL

Finally, after several years, Patrick found his way back to a joyful reunion with his family in Britain. Sometime after this Patrick had a dream, similar to the Apostle Paul's Macedonian call, as he related in his *Confessions*:

> "In the depth of the night, I saw a man named Victoricus coming as if from Ireland, with innumerable letters; and he gave me one of these, and I read the heading of the letter which ran, 'The Cry of the Irish,' and while I was reading out the be-

Patrick bids farewell to his family.

ginning of the letter, I thought that at that very moment I heard the voice of those who were beside
the wood of Focluth, near the western sea; and this
is what they called out:' Please, holy boy, come
and walk among us again.' Their cry pierced to my
very heart, and I could read no more; and so I
awoke." [42]

Patrick decided to leave his family and prepare for the
ministry. His mission did not happen all at once, as he first had to
study many years, be ordained, and gain the support of the Church
leaders for his calling to Ireland. Traveling to Auxerre in Gaul, he
studied under Germanus, the Bishop at Auxerre, France.[43] Even so,
his superiors were wary of his ability for such a mission. Records
indicate that Pope Celesine I sent a bishop, named Palladius, to Ireland around A.D. 431, but according to scholars, he was believed
to have been martyred within the year. At long last, the decision
was made to allow Patrick to go in his place.[44]

Saint Patrick

LOVE YOUR ENEMIES

Patrick was over 40 years old when he finally was allowed to pursue the vision in his heart. He crossed the stormy sea and arrived in Ireland around the year 432 A.D. with a band of twelve brave monks, probably at the mouth of the Vantry River near Wicklow Head.

To get a historical perspective of what was happening in Europe at this time, Patrick's voyage took place about twenty-two years after Rome was sacked the first time by the Visigoths, and about twenty-two years before it was sacked the second time by the Vandals. Attila the Hun, with his hordes of murdering and pillaging tribesman, were massacring all across Europe.

For the next 30 years, Patrick labored in Ireland, bring people from superstitions to the worship of God. Patrick wrote:

Missionaries crossing the sea of the cold North Atlantic.

"I dwell among gentiles....in the midst of pagan barbarians, worshipers of idols, and of unclean things."[45]

It can be said that Patrick truly followed the example of Jesus, as he forgave those who persecuted him, and set out to love the enemies who had enslaved him.

COURAGEOUS FAITH

After they landed and prayed, they were immediately met with opposition from the Druids. Patrick decided to head inland to Dalriada, to the home of his old master, Milchu, but, as the story goes, he was met by a chieftain named Dichu, who attempted to prevent his advance. As Dichu drew his sword to smite Patrick, "his arm became rigid as a statue and continued so until he declared himself obedient to Patrick....Dichu asked for instructions and made a gift of a large sabhall (barn)....This was the first sanctuary dedicated by Patrick... and the hallowed site retains the name Sabhall (pronounced Saul) to the present day."[46]

Upon reaching his destination, to his dismay, Patrick "found that Milchu had been killed in a battle with a neighboring tribe and his home was blackened with fire and in ruins."[47] Had Patrick not obeyed the inner voice of the Lord years earlier and escaped, he possibly would have been killed.[48]

R.J. Unstead, in his book *People in History-From Caractacus to Alfred* (London, Transworld Publishers, Ltd., 1975), described:

"Some of the wild Irish threw stones at the monks and tried to drive them away, but Patrick made peace with them and led them to the Hall of the greatest chief in those parts. This chief was feasting with his warriors and Druids, when a messenger rushed in to say that strangers had arrived. In the long, smoky hall the noise and singing ceased as the little party of quiet, calm men entered. One of them

Saint Patrick

Patrick in the hall of the Irish chieftain.

People in History—From Caractacus to Alfred, R.J. Unstead, Carousel Books, Transworld Publishers Ltd, Great Britain

was carrying a tall cross. The chief stared curiously at them, for visitors were rarely seen in this distant land, and he asked who they were and where they had come from.

"Lifting his hand, Patrick began to speak to them in their own language (which he had learn while a slave):

'We are men of God,' he said. 'We have come to bring you good news – the news of Jesus, the Son of God, and of his love and goodness to us all.'

"As he spoke to them, the fierce warriors saw that here was a man who was not only filled with love for all men, but who was without fear. So they let him speak, and they listened to his message.

"The Druids were angry and alarmed at this new religion, but the chief became Patrick's friend. He was baptized a Christian, and he gave the monks a piece of land on which they built their first wooden church."[49]

This began Patrick's method of first winning the leaders to Christianity, then their subjects would follow.

The *Encyclopedia Britannica* stated that Patrick challenged the:

"royal authority by lighting the Paschal fire on the hill Slane on the night of Easter Eve. It chanced to be

Croagh Patrick (Eagle Mountain), where legend holds Patrick fasted there 40 days

Saint Patrick

the occasion of a pagan festival at Tara, during which no fire might be kindled until the royal fire had been lit."[50]

As the flames of Patrick's fire illuminated the countryside, King Loigaire (King Leary) is said to have exclaimed:

"If we do not extinguish this flame it will sweep over all Ireland."[51]

Mary Cagney, in her article "Patrick the Saint" (Christianity Today, Issue 60), wrote:

then rung a bell to chase the snakes or demons out of Ireland.

"Predictably, Patrick faced the most opposition from the Druids, who practiced magic, were skilled in secular learning (especially law and history) and advised Irish kings. Biographies of the saint are replete with stories of Druids who 'wished to kill holy Patrick.'

"'Daily, I expect murder, fraud or captivity,' Patrick wrote, 'but I fear none of these things because of the promises of heaven. I have cast myself into the hands of God almighty who rules everywhere.'....

"Indeed, Patrick almost delighted in taking risks for the gospel. 'I must take this decision disregarding risks involved and make known the gifts of God and his everlasting consolation. Neither must we fear any such risk in faithfully preaching God's name boldly in every place, so that even after my death, a spiritual legacy may be left for my brethren and my children.'....

"Patrick was as fully convinced as the Celts that the power of the Druids was real, but he brought news of a stronger power. The famous Lorica (or 'Patrick's Breastplate'), a prayer of protection, may not have been written by Patrick (at least in its current form), but it expresses perfectly Patrick's confidence in God to protect him from 'every fierce merciless force that may come upon my body and soul; against incantations of false prophets, against black laws of paganism, against false laws of heresy, against deceit of idolatry, against spells of women and smiths and druids.'

"According to legend, it worked. The King, Loiguire, set up a trap to kill Patrick, but as the bishop came near, all the king could see was a deer. (Thus the Breastplate has also been known as the Deer's Cry.)...

"On biographer from the late 600's, Muirchu', described Patrick challenging Druids to contests at Tara…The custom was that whoever lit a fire before the king on that night of the year [Easter's eve] would be put to death. Patrick lit the paschal fire before the king on the hill of Slane. The people saw Patrick's fire throughout the plain, and the king ordered 27 chariots to go and seize Patrick....

"Seeing that the impious heathen were about to attack him, Patrick rose and said clearly and loudly,

'May God come up to scatter his enemies, and may those who hate him flee from his face.' By this disaster, caused by Patrick's curse in the king's presence because of the king's order, seven times seven men fell…. And the king driven by fear, came and bent his knees before the holy man….

"[The next day], in display of magic, a Druid

Slide file, Dublin, Christian History, Carol Stream, IL

Statue of Patrick near Croagh Patrick
Carbon dating of church ruins on the summit date to Patrick's time,
adding support to the legend of him fasting there.

invoked demons and brought about a dark fog over the land. Patrick said to the druid, 'Cause the fog to disperse.' But he was unable to do it. Patrick prayed and gave his blessing, and suddenly the fog cleared and the sun shone.... And through the prayers of Patrick the flames of fire consumed the druid.

"And the king was greatly enraged at Patrick because of the death of his druid. Patrick said to the king. 'If you do not believe now, you will die on the spot for the wrath of God descends on your head.'

"The king summoned his council and said, 'It is better for me to believe than to die.' And he believed as did many others that day."[52]

DANGERS

Patrick then began preaching all over Ireland, destroying idols, and encountering stiff opposition from the druids. Twelve times he faced life-threatening situations, including a harrowing kidnapping in which he was bound in chains and sentenced to die during a two week captivity.[53]

Patrick faced trials and dangers, as he wrote in his *Confession*:

"Regardless of danger I must make known the gift of God and everlasting consolation, without fear....

"And I was not worthy...that after my misfortunes and so great difficulties, after my captivity, after the lapse of so many years, He should give me so great a grace in behalf of that nation...

"I must not, however, hide God's gift which He bestowed upon me in the land of my captivity; because then I earnestly sought Him, and there I found Him, and He saved me from all evil....

"I give unwearied thanks to God, who kept me faithful in the day of my temptation... to Christ my Lord, who saved me out of all my troubles.... I constantly exalt and magnify Thy name among the

Saint Patrick

The World Book Encyclopedia - In Eighteen Volumes (Chicago, IL: Field Enterprises, Inc., 1957), Vol. 13, p. 6142.

heathens wherever I may be, and not only in good days but also in tribulations

"It would be tedious to give a detailed account of all my labours or even a part of them. Let me tell you briefly how the merciful God often freed me from slavery and from twelve dangers in which my life was at stake---not to mention numerous plots, which I cannot express in words; for I do not want to bore my readers. But God is my witness, who knows all things even before they come to pass, as He used to forewarn even me, poor wretch that I am, of many things by a divine message."[54]

"I came to the people of Ireland to preach the Gospel, and to suffer insult from the unbelievers...I am prepared to give even my life without hesitation and most gladly for His name, and it is there that I wish to spend it until I die...

"For many tried to prevent this my mission; they would even talk to each other behind my back and say: `Why does this fellow throw himself into danger among enemies who have no knowledge of God?'...

"I went to you and everywhere for your sake in many dangers, even to the farthest districts, beyond which there lived nobody and where nobody had ever come to baptize...

"Even so they laid hands on me and my companions, and on that day they eagerly wished to kill me; but my time had not yet come. And everything they found with us they took away, and me they put in irons; and on the fourteenth day the Lord delivered me from their power, and our belongings were returned to us because of God and our dear friends whom we had seen before."

"Daily I expect murder, fraud, or captivity, or whatever it may be; but I fear none of these things because of the promises of heaven. I have cast myself into the hands of God Almighty, who rules everywhere, as the prophet says: Cast thy thought upon God, and He shall sustain thee."

"I beg Him to grant me that I may shed my

blood with those exiles and captives for His name, even though I should be denied a grave, or my body be woefully torn to pieces limb by limb by hounds or wild beasts, or the fowls of the air devour it. I am firmly convinced that if this should happen to me, I would have gained my soul together with my body, because on that day without doubt we shall rise in the brightness of the sun, that is, in the glory of Christ Jesus our Redeemer."[55]

Legend holds that Patrick rang a large bell on top of Croagh Patrick to scare away Ireland's snakes or demons

POWER OF PRAYER

Many times Patrick demonstrated the power of God as greater than the druid magic. This convinced the powerful druid chieftains to convert to Christianity, especially in the areas of Tara, Croagh Patrick, and Armagh, where Patrick established his archiepiscopal see. One story tells of how Patrick was in an area plagued with snakes, and that after he prayed, the serpents left the area and were driven into the sea.

PERSECUTORS TO PRAISERS

Thomas Cahill, author of "How the Irish Saved Civilization" (Doubleday, 1995), stated that the Druids':

"view of god, that lies behind these imprecations [human sacrifices], is of an arbitrary trickster, a bad parent who can be coaxed, flattered, and manipulated. If belief in such a god is strong and primitive enough, it is easy to see how it can lead to human sacrifice: 'Here, take him, not me!'....Patrick declared that such sacrifices were no longer needed. Christ had died once for all. I'd bet he quoted Paul, his model, who in his letter to the church at Phillippi recited this mysterious poem about sacrifice....'Though he possessed divine estate, He was not jealous to retain equality with God. He cast off his inheritance. He took the nature of a slave and walked as Man among men. He emptied himself to the last and was obedient to death – to death upon a cross. And, therefore, god has raised him up and God has given him the Name-which-is-above-all-names, that at the name of Jesus all in heaven high shall bow the knee and all the earth and depths."[56]

Druid bards converted and became Christians. They were renown for singing beautiful praises to God

The bold faith and miracles that accompanied Patrick resulted in the druids as a class losing their influence, and eventually becoming Christians themselves. The druids, who were also a sort of minstrel class, traveled around as bards or musicians. In time they became baptized and used their harps for playing praises to God, so beautiful that it was acclaimed that angels in heaven bent down to listen. The harp has since been a badge of Ireland.

PATRICK - THE FOUNDER

Patrick, made converts of all classes of society: kings, aristocracy, peasants and druids. "As kings converted, they gave their sons to Patrick in an old Irish custom for educating and 'fostering.'…Eventually, the sons and daughters of the Irish were persuaded to become monks and nuns."[57]

Patrick baptizing the Druids

Irish monastery with stone huts, palisade and tower

Ireland was a rural country and as yet did not have towns. Patrick would travel from kingdom to kingdom, concentrating his effort on the country's one hundred or so tribal kings, for when a king became a Christian, his people would follow his example. Once a number of pagans were converted, Patrick would build a church, ordain deacons and ministers, and leave them in charge. Many chieftains were generous enough to grant a site for a church and a monastery, which grew to function as a missionary station. Patrick placed a great emphasis on spiritual growth and gave converts intense training in the Scriptures. "Before departing, Patrick gave the new converts (or their pastors) a compendium of Christian doctrine and the canons (rules)."[58]

A key to Patrick's success was that he set up each church and monastery as an independent unit, leaving the power in the hands of the abbots, rather than setting up an hierarchical structure. The bishops were selected by the monastic clergy on whom they were dependent.

PATRICK - THE ABOLITIONIST

Patrick was the first Christian to speak out strongly against slavery, having himself been a victim. "Scholars agree he is the

Saint Patrick

genuine author of a letter excommunicating a British tyrant, Coroti-cus, who carried off some of Patrick's converts into slavery. 'Ravenous wolves have gulped down the Lord's own flock which was flourishing in Ireland,' he wrote, 'and the whole church cries out and laments for its sons and daughters.' He called Coroticus' deed 'wicked, so horrible, so unutterable,' and told him to repent and free the converts.... Within his lifetime (or shortly thereafter), Patrick ended the entire Irish slave trade."[59]

HUMBLE

From his writings, Patrick strug-gled with feelings of inferiority, due to his never having finished his formal Latin education on account of his kidnapping as a child. He continually acknowledged this inferiority, as seen in his Confessions:

Patrick over snake

"Patrick the sinner, an unlearned man to be sure... I had long had it in mind to write, but up to now I have hesitated. I was afraid lest I should fall under the judgment of men's tongues be-cause I am not as well read as oth-ers.... As a youth, nay, almost as a boy not able to speak, I was taken captive... Hence to-day I blush and fear exceedingly to reveal my lack of education; for I am unable to tell my story to those versed in the art of concise writing---in such a way, I mean, as my spirit and mind long to do, and so that the sense of my words expresses what I feel."[60]

And in his letter, Epistle to Coroticus, he begins:

"I, Patrick, a sinner, very badly educated."[61]

Remains of Franciscan friary of Armagh. By tradition Patrick was bishop of Armagh

Patrick turned his weakness into a strength. Instead of writing complicated Latin theological works, he resorted to teaching with illustrations. So well did people remember his illustrations, that even today Ireland is known for the Three Leaf Clover, which Patrick used to explain the Holy Trinity. (Shamrock is anglicized from Seamrog, which means trefoil or three-leaved.)[62]

CHARACTER

Patrick also encouraged the converts to quickly become involved in the ministry. He also refused the gifts of many, lest any breath of scandal should arise.

In his *Confession*, Patrick wrote:

> "And many gifts were offered to me in sorrow and tears, and I offended the donors, much against the wishes of some of my seniors; but, guided by God, in no way did I agree with them or acquiesce."[63]

WOMEN

Patrick encouraged women to be involved, although he was cautious in his relationship with them, as he wrote:

"Among others, a blessed Irishwoman of noble birth, beautiful, full-grown, whom I had baptized, came to us after some days for a particular reason: she told us that she had received a message from a messenger of God, and he admonished her to be a virgin of Christ and draw near to God. Thanks be to God, on the sixth day after this she most laudably and eagerly chose what all virgins of Christ do. Not that their fathers agree with them: no---they often ever suffer persecution and undeserved reproaches from their parents; and yet their number is ever increasing. How many have been reborn there so as to be of our kind, I do not know---not to mention widows and those who practice continence."[64]

UNDER INVESTIGATION

Mary Cagney, author of "Patrick the Saint" (Christianity History, Issue 60, wrote:

"At one point, his ecclesiastical elders in Britain sent a deputation to investigate his mission. A number of concerns were brought up, including a rash moment (unspecified) sin from his youth. He Confession, in fact, was written in response to this investigation. Reeling from accusations, Patrick drew strength from God: 'Indeed he bore me up, though I was trampled underfoot in such a way. For although I was put down and shamed, not too much harm came to me.'"[65]

In his *Confession*, Patrick wrote:

"And when I was attacked by a number of my seniors who came forth and brought up my sins against my laborious episcopate, on that day indeed was I struck so that I might have fallen now and for eternity; but the Lord graciously spared the stranger and sojourner for His name and came mightily to my help in this affliction Verily, not slight was the shame and blame that fell upon me!...

"As cause for proceeding against me they found---after thirty years!---a confession I had made before I was a deacon. In the anxiety of my troubled mind I confided to my dearest friend what I had done in my boyhood one day, nay, in one hour, because I was not yet strong. I know not, God knoweth--- whether I was then fifteen years old: and I did not believe in the living God, nor did I so from my childhood, but lived in death and unbelief until I was severely chastised and really humiliated, by hunger and nakedness, and that daily....

"On that day, then, when I was rejected by those referred to and mentioned above, in that night I saw a vision of the night. There was a writing without honour against my face, and at the same time I heard God's voice saying to me: `We have seen with displeasure the face of Deisignatus' (thus revealing his name).... He who toucheth you toucheth as it were the apple of my eye'...

"But the more am I sorry for my dearest friend that we had to hear what he said. To him I had confided my very soul! And I was told by some of the brethren before that defense---at which I was not present, nor was I in Britain, nor was it suggested by me---that he would stand up for me in my absence. He had even said to me in person: `Look, you should be raised to the rank of bishop!'---of which I was not worthy. But whence did it come to him afterwards that he let me down before all, good and evil, and publicly, in a matter in which he had favoured me before spontaneously and gladly---and not he alone, but the Lord, who is greater than all?"[66]

Patrick climbing the hill known as Croagh Patrick

Saint Patrick Climbs Croagh Patrick by Margaret Clarke/ Hugh Lane Municipal Gallery of Modern Art, Dublin, Christian History, Carol Stream, Illinois, Issue 60

MOTIVATION

After thirty years of ministry, Patrick revealed his motivation, "I fear to lose the labor which I began lest God would note me as guilty."[67] In his *Confession*, he wrote:

> "Wherefore, then, even if I wished to leave them and go to Britain---and how I would have loved to go to my country and my parents, and also to Gaul in order to visit the brethren and to see the face of the saints of my Lord! God knows it! that I much desired it; but I am bound by the Spirit, who gives evidence against me if I do this, telling me that I shall be guilty; and I am afraid of losing the labour which I have begun---nay, not I, but Christ the Lord who bade me come here and stay with them for the rest of my life, if the Lord will, and will guard me from every evil way that I may not sin before Him....
>
> "Wherefore may God never permit it to happen to me that I should lose His people which He purchased in the utmost parts of the world. I pray to God to give me perseverance and to deign that I be a faithful witness to Him to the end of my life."[68]

TRIUMPH

Patrick's success was seen through the over 300 churches he founded and the over 120,000 converts he baptized.[69] Two centuries after his death, in A.D. 664, Patrick was bestowed the title of Saint after the Synod of Whitby Abbey, where King Oswy of Northumbria agreed to come under the authority of the Roman Catholic Church.[70] Patrick's legacy undeniably impacted the world, even up to the present time. He so thoroughly implanted the missionary vision, that during the 6th and 7th centuries, it was the Celtic missionaries who re-evangelized Western Europe.

LEGACY

One of the people Patrick baptized was a leader named Conall, whose grandson, Columba (which means "dove"), became the great Irish missionary to Scotland and England.[71] Of royal birth, legend tells that Columba, an eager student, supposedly made an unauthorized copy of Jerome's version of the Psalter, which had been

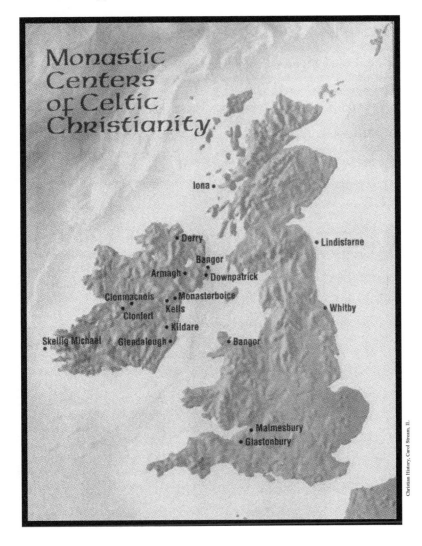

Christian History, Carol Stream, IL.

brought back from Rome. When his teacher, Finnian, demanded it returned, Columba refused. This led Finnian to seek judgment against Columba from the high king of Tara. Unfortunately, this escalated into a battle in which 3,001 men died. Columba was so remorseful that he determined to save as many souls. He went into exile and in A.D. 563, founded a monastery on the desolate island of Iona in the cold north sea between Ireland and Scotland.

Columba's monastery on the Island of Iona, northwest of Scotland

Shore of Island of Iona, with the Abbey Church in background.

Saint Patrick

Photograph by Peter Wyatt, *Great Leaders of the Christian Church,* Moody Press, Chicago

Stained glass portrait of Columba ("Columcille"),
from the abbey on the Island of Iona.

Columba's monastery at Iona became a missionary training base from which to evangelize the Scots and Picts. Columba visited the banks of Loch Ness, where he converted King Brude of the Northern Picts. His ministry "known as much a religion of miracles as of ethics and creeds,"[72] is filled with reports, such as how he "faced down the king of Picts through his power, blasting him with loud psalms, throwing wide his strong oak doors, and besting the magic of the king's druids. He even defeats wild animals: a fierce boar drops dead on the spot, and a strange monster on Loch Ness runs from his power."[73] The monastic system Columba established of

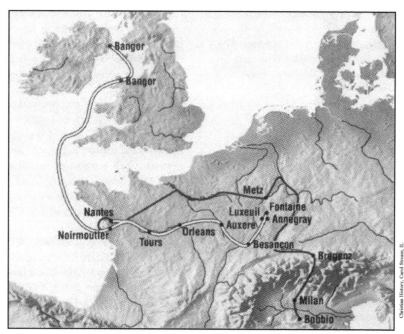

Christian History, Carol Stream, IL.

Columbanus' missionary journeys in Europe

"work, prayer and reading," set an example for later orders, such as the Cistercians and Carthusians.

The monks that were trained at Iona followed Patrick's example of leaving his home country to spread the gospel. Many traveled into the continent of Europe to evangelized the new pagan tribes which had overrun the Roman Empire.

One such missionary was Columbanus (A.D. 543-615), who took the gospel to the Rhineland, to the Franks, the Germanic tribes, even across the Alps into Italy. He founded the abbeys of Luxeuil, Fontaine, and Bobbio in northern Italy, which grew into cultural centers of great importance. Columbanus and his disciples founded at least 60, and possibly over 100 monasteries throughout Europe.[74]

Thus, the influence of Patrick's life was multiplied many times over through those he converted. Patrick wrote in his *Confession*:

"I must make this choice, regardless of danger I must make known the gift of God and everlasting consolation, without fear and frankly I must spread everywhere the name of God so that after my decease I may leave a bequest to my brethren and sons whom I have baptized in the Lord---so many thousands of people."[75]

Another translation reads:

> "I must take this decision disregarding risks involved and make known the gifts of God and his everlasting consolation. Neither must we fear any such risk in faithfully preaching God's name boldly in every place, so that even after my death, a spiritual legacy may be left for my brethren and my children."[76]

DEATH

Patrick died on March 17, possibly around 461 A.D., near his first wooden church. Described as the man who "found Ireland all heathen and left it all Christian,"[77] Patrick gave God the glory for all his accomplishments, as he wrote in his *Confessions*:

> "But I pray those who believe and fear God, whosoever has deigned to scan or accept this document, composed in Ireland by Patrick the sinner, an unlearned man to be sure, that none should ever say that it was my ignorance that accomplished any small thing which I did or showed in accordance with God's will; but judge ye, and let it be most truly believed, that it was the gift of God. And this is my confession before I die."[78]

Patrick used three-leaf clover to teach the Trinity

Slide file, Dublin, Christian History, Carol Stram, IL.

Stone placed outside Downpatrick Cathedral to mark Patrick's grave

PATRICK'S BREASTPLATE

(Also known as the *Shield of Patrick*, or the *Deer's Cry*)
Paraphrased by Mrs. Cecil Frances Alexander

I bind unto myself today
The strong name of the Trinity,
By invocation of the same,
The Three in One, the One in Three.

Saint Patrick

Each July, on the last Sunday, nearly 30,000 pilgrims climb the 2,710-foot summit of Croagh Patrick, where Patrick fasted 40 days and nights

I bind this day to me for ever
By power of faith, Christ's incarnation;
His baptism in the Jordan river;
His death on the cross for my salvation.
His bursting from the spiced tomb;
His riding up the heavenly way;
His coming at the day of doom;
I bind unto myself today.

Saint Patrick

I bind unto myself today
The power of God to hold and lead,
His eye to watch, his might to stay,
His ear to harken to my need;
The wisdom of my God to teach,
His hand to guide, his shield to ward,
The Word of God to give me speech,
His heavenly host to be my guard.

Saint Patrick

Against all Satan's spells and wiles,
Against false words of heresy,
Against the knowledge that defiles,
Against the heart's idolatry,
Against the wizard's evil craft,
Against the death-wound and the burning,
The choking wave, the poison'd shaft,
Protect me, Christ, till thy returning.

Clonmacnois Monastery, County Offaly, Ireland, after Viking attacks.

Saint Patrick

Christ be with me, Christ within me,
Christ behind me, Christ before me,
Christ beside me, Christ to win me;
Christ to comfort and restore me;
Christ beneath me, Christ above me,
Christ in quiet, Christ in danger,
Christ in hearts of all that love me,
Christ in mouth of friend and stranger.

I bind unto myself the name,
The strong name of the Trinity,
By invocation of the same,
The Three in One, and One in Three,
Of whom all nature hath creation,
Eternal Father, Spirit, Word;
Praise to the God of my salvation;
Salvation is of Christ the Lord![79]

Monastery at Ardmore, County Waterford, after Viking attacks.

Remains of the Whitby Abbey, famous for the synod of A.D. 664

Monastery on the lonely Island of Farne.

Saint Patrick

Irish Tourist Board. Photo by P. Tutty, *Eerdmans' Handbook to the History of Christianity*, Grand Rapids, MI.

Monastery on the isolated Island of Skellig Michael, County Kerry, Ireland

Saint Patrick

Slide File, Dublin, Christian History, Carol Stream, Il.

Slide File, Dublin, Christian History, Carol Stream, Il.

Stairs to the 460-foot-high peak of Skellig Michael

Saint Patrick

APPENDIX

THE CONFESSION OF PATRICK

Translated from the Latin by Ludwig Bieler

I am Patrick, a sinner, most unlearned, the least of all the faithful, and utterly despised by many. My father was Calpornius, a deacon, son of Potitus, a priest, of the village Bannavem Taburniæ; he had a country seat nearby, and there I was taken captive.

I was then about sixteen years of age. I did not know the true God. I was taken into captivity to Ireland with many thousands of people---and deservedly so, because we turned away from God, and did not keep His commandments, and did not obey our priests, who used to remind us of our salvation.

And the Lord brought over us the wrath of his anger and scattered us among many nations, even unto the utmost part of the earth, where now my littleness is placed among strangers.

And there the Lord opened the sense of my unbelief that I might at last remember my sins and be converted with all my heart to the Lord my God, who had regard for my abjection, and mercy on my youth and ignorance, and watched over me before I knew Him, and before I was able to distinguish between good and evil, and guarded me, and comforted me as would a father his son.

Hence I cannot be silent---nor, indeed, is it expedient---about the great benefits and the great grace which the lord has deigned to bestow upon me in the land of my captivity; for this we can give to God in return after having been chastened by Him, to exalt and praise His wonders before every nation that is anywhere under the heaven.

Because there is no other God, nor ever was, nor will be, than God the Father unbegotten, without beginning, from whom is all beginning, the Lord of the universe, as we have been taught; and His son Jesus Christ, whom we declare to have always been with the Father, spiritually and ineffably begotten by the Father before the beginning of the world, before all beginning; and by Him are made all things visible and invisible.

He was made man, and, having defeated death, was received into heaven by the Father; and He hath given Him all power over all names in heaven, on earth, and under the earth, and every tongue shall confess to Him that Jesus Christ is Lord and God, in whom we believe, and whose advent we expect soon to be, judge of the living and of the dead, who will render to every man according to his deeds;

and He has poured forth upon us abundantly the Holy Spirit, the gift and pledge of immortality, who makes those who believe and obey sons of God and joint heirs with Christ; and Him do we confess and adore, one God in the Trinity of the Holy Name.

For He Himself has said through the Prophet: Call upon me in the day of thy trouble, and I will deliver thee, and thou shalt glorify me. And again He says: It is honourable to reveal and confess the works of God.

Although I am imperfect in many things, I nevertheless wish that my brethren and kinsmen should know what sort of person I am, so that they may understand my heart's desire.

I know well the testimony of my Lord, who in the Psalm declares: Thou wilt destroy them that speak a lie. And again He says: The mouth that belieth killeth the soul. And the same Lord says in the Gospel: Every idle word that men shall speak, they shall render an account for it on the day of judgement.

And so I should dread exceedingly, with fear and trembling, this sentence on that day when no one will be able to escape or hide, but we all, without exception, shall have to give an account even of our smallest sins before the judgement of the Lord Christ.

For this reason I had in mind to write, but hesitated until now; I was afraid of exposing myself to the talk of men, because I have not studied like the others, who thoroughly imbibed law and Sacred Scripture, and never had to change from the language of their childhood days, but were able to make it still more perfect.

In our case, what I had to say had to be translated into a tongue foreign to me, as can be easily proved from the savour of my writing, which betrays how little instruction and training I have had in the art of words; for, so says Scripture, by the tongue will be discovered the wise man, and understanding, and knowledge, and the teaching of truth.

But of what help is an excuse, however true, especially if combined with presumption, since now, in my old age, I strive for something that I did not acquire in youth? It was my sins that prevented me from fixing in my mind what before I had barely read through. But who believes me, though I should repeat what I started out with?

As a youth, nay, almost as a boy not able to speak, I was taken captive, before I knew what to pursue and what to avoid. Hence to-day I blush and fear exceedingly to reveal my lack of education; for I am unable to tell my story to those versed in the art of concise writing---in such a way, I mean, as my spirit and mind long to do, and so that the sense of my words expresses what I feel.

But if indeed it had been given to me as it was given to others, then I would not be silent because of my desire of thanksgiving; and if perhaps some people think me arrogant for doing so in spite of my lack of knowledge and my slow tongue, it is, after all, written: The stammering tongues shall quickly learn to speak peace.

How much more should we earnestly strive to do this, we, who are, so Scripture says, a letter of Christ for salvation unto the utmost part of the earth, and, though not an eloquent one, yet... written in your hearts, not with ink, but with the spirit of the living God! And again the Spirit witnesses that even rusticity was created by the Highest.

Whence I, once rustic, exiled, unlearned, who does not know how to provide for the future, this at least I know most certainly that before I was humiliated I was like a stone Lying in the deep mire;

and He that is mighty came and in His mercy lifted me up, and raised me aloft, and placed me on the top of the wall.

And therefore I ought to cry out aloud and so also render something to the Lord for His great benefits here and in eternity---benefits which the mind of men is unable to appraise.

Wherefore, then, be astonished, ye great and little that fear God, and you men of letters on your estates, listen and pore over this. Who was it that roused up me, the fool that I am, from the midst of those who in the eyes of men are wise, and expert in law, and powerful in word and in everything?

And He inspired me---me, the outcast of this world---before others, to be the man (if only I could!) who, with fear and reverence and without blame, should faithfully serve the people to whom the love of Christ conveyed and gave me for the duration of my life, if I should be worthy; yes indeed, to serve them humbly and sincerely.

In the light, therefore, of our faith in the Trinity I must make this choice, regardless of danger I must make known the gift of God and everlasting consolation, without fear and frankly I must spread everywhere the name of God so that after my decease I may leave a bequest to my brethren and sons whom I have baptized in the Lord---so many thousands of people.

And I was not worthy, nor was I such that the Lord should grant this to His servant; that after my misfortunes and so great difficulties, after my captivity, after the lapse of so many years, He should give me so great a grace in behalf of that nation---a thing which once, in my youth, I never expected nor thought of.

But after I came to Ireland---every day I had to tend sheep, and many times a day I prayed---the love of God and His fear came to me more and more, and my faith was strengthened. And my spirit was moved so that in a single day I would say as many as a hundred prayers, and almost as many in the night, and this even when I was staying in the woods and on the mountains; and I used to get up for prayer before daylight, through snow, through frost, through rain, and I felt no harm, and there was no sloth in me---as I now see, because the spirit within me was then fervent.

And there one night I heard in my sleep a voice saying to me: `It is well that you fast, soon you will go to your own country.' And again, after a short while, I heard a voice saying to me: `See, your ship is ready.'

And it was not near, but at a distance of perhaps two hundred miles, and I had never been there, nor did I know a living soul there; and then I took to flight, and I left the man with whom I had stayed for six years. And I went in the strength of God who directed my way to my good, and I feared nothing until I came to that ship.

And the day that I arrived the ship was set afloat, and I said that I was able to pay for my passage with them. But the captain was not pleased, and with indignation he answered harshly: `It is of no use for you to ask us to go along with us.' And when I heard this, I left them in order to return to the hut where I was staying.

And as I went, I began to pray; and before I had ended my prayer, I heard one of them shouting behind me, `Come, hurry, we shall take you on in good faith; make friends with us in whatever way you like.' And so on that day I refused to suck their breasts for fear of God, but rather hoped they would come to the faith of Jesus Christ, because they were pagans. And thus I had my way with them, and we set sail at once.

And after three days we reached land, and for twenty-eight days we traveled through deserted country. And they lacked food, and hunger overcame them; and the next day the captain said to me: `Tell me, Christian: you say that your God is great and all-powerful; why, then, do you not pray for us? As you can see, we are suffering from hunger; it is unlikely indeed that we shall ever see a human being again.'

I said to them full of confidence: `Be truly converted with all your heart to the Lord my God, because nothing is impossible for Him, that this day He may send you food on your way until you be satisfied; for He has abundance everywhere.' And, with the help of God, so it came to pass: suddenly a herd of pigs appeared on the road before our eyes, and they killed many of them; and there they stopped for two nights and fully recovered their strength, and their hounds received their fill for many of them had grown weak and were half-dead along the way.

And from that day they had plenty of food. They also found wild honey, and offered some of it to me, and one of them said: `This we offer in sacrifice.' Thanks be to God, I tasted none of it.

That same night, when I was asleep, Satan assailed me violently, a thing I shall remember as long as I shall be in this body. And he fell upon me like a huge rock, and I could not stir a limb. But whence came it into my mind, ignorant as I am, to call upon Elias?

And meanwhile I saw the sun rise in the sky, and while I was shouting `Elias! Elias' with all my might, suddenly the splendour of that sun fell on me and immediately freed me of all misery.

And I believe that I was sustained by Christ my Lord, and that His Spirit was even then crying out in my behalf, and I hope it will be so on the day of my tribulation, as is written in the Gospel: On that day, the Lord declares, it is not you that speak, but the Spirit of your Father that speaketh in you.

And once again, after many years, I fell into captivity. On that first night I stayed with them, I heard a divine message saying to me: `Two months will you be with them.' And so it came to pass: on the sixtieth night thereafter the Lord delivered me out of their hands.

Also on our way God gave us food and fire and dry weather every day, until, on the tenth day, we met people. As I said above, we traveled twenty-eight days through deserted country, and the night that we met people we had no food left.

And again after a few years I was in Britain with my people. who received me as their son, and sincerely besought me that now at last, having suffered so many hardships, I should not leave them and go elsewhere.

And there I saw in the night the vision of a man, whose name was Victoricus, coming as it were from Ireland, with countless letters.

And he gave me one of them, and I read the opening words of the letter, which were, `The voice of the Irish'; and as I read the beginning of the letter I thought that at the same moment I heard their voice---they were those beside the Wood of Voclut, which is near the Western Sea---and thus did they cry out as with one mouth: `We ask thee, boy, come and walk among us once more.'

And I was quite broken in heart, and could read no further, and so I woke up. Thanks be to God, after many years the Lord gave to them according to their cry.

And another night---whether within me, or beside me, I know not, God knoweth---they called me most unmistakably with words which I heard but could not understand, except that at the end of the prayer He spoke thus: `He that has laid down His life for thee, it is He that speaketh in thee'; and so I awoke full of joy.

And again I saw Him praying in me, and I was as it were within my body, and I heard Him above me, that is, over the inward man, and there He prayed mightily with groanings. And all the time I was astonished, and wondered, and thought with myself who it could be that prayed in me.

But at the end of the prayer He spoke, saying that He was the Spirit; and so I woke up, and remembered the Apostle saying: The Spirit helpeth the infirmities of our prayer. For we know not what we should pray for as we ought; but the Spirit Himself asketh for us with unspeakable groanings, which cannot be expressed in words; and again: The Lord our advocate asketh for us.

And when I was attacked by a number of my seniors who came forth and brought up my sins against my laborious episcopate, on that day indeed was I struck so that I might have fallen now and for eternity; but the Lord graciously spared the stranger and sojourner for His name and came mightily to my help in this affliction Verily, not slight was the shame and blame that fell upon me! I ask God that it may not be reckoned to them as sin.

As cause for proceeding against me they found---after thirty years!---a confession I had made before I was a deacon. In the anxiety of my troubled mind I confided to my dearest friend what I had done in my boyhood one day, nay, in one hour, because I was not yet strong.

Saint Patrick

I know not, God knoweth---whether I was then fifteen years old: and I did not believe in the living God, nor did I so from my childhood, but lived in death and unbelief until I was severely chastised and really humiliated, by hunger and nakedness, and that daily.

On the other hand, I did not go to Ireland of my own accord, not until I had nearly perished; but this was rather for my good, for thus was I purged by the Lord; and He made me fit so that I might be now what was once far from me that I should care and labour for the salvation of others, whereas then I did not even care about myself.

On that day, then, when I was rejected by those referred to and mentioned above, in that night I saw a vision of the night. There was a writing without honour against my face, and at the same time I heard God's voice saying to me: `We have seen with displeasure the face of Deisignatus' (thus revealing his name). He did not say, `Thou hast seen.' but `We have seen.' as if He included Himself, as He sayeth: He who toucheth you toucheth as it were the apple of my eye.

Therefore I give Him thanks who hath strengthened me in everything, as He did not frustrate the journey upon which I had decided, and the work which I had learned from Christ my Lord; but I rather felt after this no little strength, and my trust was proved right before God and men.

And so I say boldly, my conscience does not blame me now or in the future: God is my witness that I have not lied in the account which I have given you.

But the more am I sorry for my dearest friend that we had to hear what he said. To him I had confided my very soul! And I was told by some of the brethren before that defense---at which I was not present, nor was I in Britain, nor was it suggested by me---that he would stand up for me in my absence. He had even said to me in person: `Look, you should be raised to the rank of bishop!'---of which I was not worthy.

But whence did it come to him afterwards that he let me down before all, good and evil, and publicly, in a matter in which he had favoured me before spontaneously and gladly---and not he alone, but the Lord, who is greater than all?

Enough of this. I must not, however, hide God's gift which He bestowed upon me in the land of my captivity; because then I earnestly sought Him, and there I found Him, and He saved me from all evil because---so I believe---of His Spirit that dwelleth in me. Again, boldly said. But God knows it, had this been said to me by a man, I had perhaps remained silent for the love of Christ.

Hence, then, I give unwearied thanks to God, who kept me faithful in the day of my temptation, so that today I can confidently offer Him my soul as a living sacrifice---to Christ my Lord, who saved me out of all my troubles. Thus I can say: `Who am I, O Lord, and to what hast Thou called me, Thou who didst assist me with such divine power that to-day I constantly exalt and magnify Thy name among the heathens wherever I may be, and not only in good days but also in tribulations?'

So indeed I must accept with equanimity whatever befalls me, be it good or evil, and always give thanks to God, who taught me to trust in Him always without hesitation, and who must have heard my prayer so that I, however ignorant I was, in the last days dared to undertake such a holy and wonderful work---thus imitating somehow those who, as the Lord once foretold, would preach His Gospel for a testimony to all nations before the end of the world. So we have seen it, and so it has been fulfilled: indeed, we are witnesses that the Gospel has been preached unto those parts beyond which there lives nobody.

Now, it would be tedious to give a detailed account of all my labours or even a part of them. Let me tell you briefly how the merciful God often freed me from slavery and from twelve dangers in which my life was at stake---not to mention numerous plots, which I cannot express in words; for I do not want to bore my readers.

But God is my witness, who knows all things even before they come to pass, as He used to forewarn even me, poor wretch that I am, of many things by a divine message.

How came I by this wisdom, which was not in me, who neither knew the number of my days nor knew what God was? Whence was given to me afterwards the gift so great, so salutary---

to know God and to love Him, although at the price of leaving my country and my parents?

And many gifts were offered to me in sorrow and tears, and I offended the donors, much against the wishes of some of my seniors; but, guided by God, in no way did I agree with them or acquiesce. It was not grace of my own, but God, who is strong in me and resists them all---as He had done when I came to the people of Ireland to preach the Gospel, and to suffer insult from the unbelievers, hearing the reproach of my going abroad, and many persecutions even unto bonds, and to give my free birth for the benefit of others; and, should I be worthy, I am prepared to give even my life without hesitation and most gladly for His name, and it is there that I wish to spend it until I die, if the Lord would grant it to me.

For I am very much God's debtor, who gave me such grace that many people were reborn in God through me and afterwards confirmed, and that clerics were ordained for them everywhere, for a people just coming to the faith, whom the Lord took from the utmost parts of the earth, as He once had promised through His prophets: To Thee the gentiles shall come from the ends of the earth and shall say: `How false are the idols that our fathers got for themselves, and there is no profit in them'; and again: `I have set Thee as a light among the gentiles, that Thou mayest be for salvation unto the utmost part of the earth.'

And there I wish to wait for His promise who surely never deceives, as He promises in the Gospel: They shall come from the east and the west, and shall sit down with Abraham and Isaac and Jacob---as we believe the faithful will come from all the world.

For that reason, therefore, we ought to fish well and diligently, as the Lord exhorts in advance and teaches, saying: Come ye after me, and I will make you to be fishers of men. And again He says through the prophets: Behold, I send many fishers and hunters, saith God, and so on.

Hence it was most necessary to spread our nets so that a great multitude and throng might be caught for God, and that there be clerics everywhere to baptize and exhort a people in need and want, as the Lord in the Gospel states, exhorts and teaches, saying: Going therefore now, teach ye all nations, baptizing them in the name of the Father, and the Son, and the Holy Spirit, teaching them to observe all things whatsoever I have commanded you: and behold I am with you all days even to the consummation of the world.

And again He says: Go ye therefore into the whole world, and preach the Gospel to every creature. He that believeth and is baptized shall be saved; but he that believeth not shall be condemned.

And again: This Gospel of the kingdom shall be preached in the whole world for a testimony to all nations, and then shall come the end.

And so too the Lord announces through the prophet, and says: And it shall come to pass, in the last days, saith the Lord, I will pour out of my Spirit upon all flesh; and your sons and your daughters shall prophesy, and your young men shall see visions, and your old men shall dream dreams. And upon my servants indeed, and upon my handmaids will I pour out in those days of my Spirit, and they shall prophesy.

And in Osee, He saith: `I will call that which was not my people, my people; ...and her that had not obtained mercy, one that hath obtained mercy. And it shall be in the place where it was said: "You are not my people," there they shall be called the sons of the living God.'

Hence, how did it come to pass in Ireland that those who never had a knowledge of God, but until now always worshipped idols and things impure, have now been made a people of the Lord, and are called sons of God, that the sons and daughters of the kings of the Irish are seen to be monks and virgins of Christ?

Among others, a blessed Irishwoman of noble birth, beautiful, full-grown, whom I had baptized, came to us after some days for a particular reason: she told us that she had received a message from a messenger of God, and he admonished her to be a virgin of Christ and draw near to God.

Thanks be to God, on the sixth day after this she most laudably and eagerly chose what all virgins of Christ do. Not that their fathers agree with them: no---they often ever suffer persecution and undeserved reproaches from their parents; and yet their number is ever increasing. How many have been reborn there so as to be of our kind, I do not know---not to mention widows and those who practice continence.

But greatest is the suffering of those women who live in slavery. All the time they have to endure terror and threats. But the Lord gave His grace to many of His maidens; for, though they are forbidden to do so, they follow Him bravely.

Wherefore, then, even if I wished to leave them and go to Britain---and how I would have loved to go to my country and my parents, and also to Gaul in order to visit the brethren and to see the face of the saints of my Lord! God knows it! that I much desired it; but I am bound by the Spirit, who gives evidence against me if I do this, telling me that I shall be guilty; and I am afraid of losing the labour which I have begun---nay, not I, but Christ the Lord who bade me come here and stay with them for the rest of my life, if the Lord will, and will guard me from every evil way that I may not sin before Him.

This, I presume, I ought to do, but I do not trust myself as long as I am in this body of death, for strong is he who daily strives to turn me away from the faith and the purity of true religion to which I have devoted myself to the end of my life to Christ my Lord.

But the hostile flesh is ever dragging us unto death, that is, towards the forbidden satisfaction of one's desires; and I know that in part I did not lead a perfect life as did the other faithful; but I acknowledge it to my! Lord, and do not blush before Him, because I lie not: from the time I came to know Him in my youth, the love of God and the fear of Him have grown in me, and up to now, thanks to the grace of God, I have kept the faith.

And let those who will, laugh and scorn---I shall not be silent; nor shall I hide the signs and wonders which the Lord has shown me many years before they came to pass, as He knows everything even before the times of the world.

Hence I ought unceasingly to give thanks to God who often pardoned my folly and my carelessness, and on more than one occasion spared His great wrath on me, who was chosen to be His helper and who was slow to do as was shown me and as the Spirit suggested. And the Lord had mercy on me thousands and thousands of times because He saw that I was ready, but that I did not know what to do in the circumstances.

For many tried to prevent this my mission; they would even talk to each other behind my back and say: `Why does this fellow throw himself into danger among enemies who have no knowledge of God?' It was not malice, but it did not appeal to them because---and to this I own myself---of my rusticity. And I did not realize at once the grace that was then in me; now I understand that I should have done so before.

Now I have given a simple account to my brethren and fellow servants who have believed me because of what I said and still say in order to strengthen and confirm your faith. Would that you, too, would strive for greater things and do better! This will be my glory, for a wise son is the glory of his father.

You know, and so does God, how I have lived among you from my youth in the true faith and in sincerity of heart. Likewise, as regards the heathen among whom I live, I have been faithful to them, and so I shall be.

God knows it, I have overreached none of them, nor would I think of doing so, for the sake of God and His Church, for fear of raising persecution against them and all of us, and for fear that through me the name of the Lord be blasphemed; for it is written: Woe to the man through whom the name of the Lord is blasphemed.

For although I be rude in all things, nevertheless I have tried somehow to keep myself safe, and that, too, for my Christian brethren, and the virgins of Christ, and the pious women who of their own accord made me gifts and laid on the altar some of their ornaments and I gave them back to them, and they were offended that I did so.

But I did it for the hope of lasting success---in order to preserve myself cautiously in everything so that they might not seize upon me or the ministry of my service, under the pretext of dishonesty, and that I would not even in the smallest matter give the infidels an opportunity to defame or defile.

When I baptized so many thousands of people, did I perhaps expect from any of them as much as half a scruple? Tell me, and I will restore it to you. Or when the Lord ordained clerics everywhere through my unworthy person and I conferred the ministry upon them free, if I asked any of them as much as the price of my shoes, speak against me and I will return it to you.

On the contrary, I spent money for you that they might receive me; and I went to you and everywhere for your sake in many dangers, even to the farthest districts, beyond which there lived nobody and where nobody had ever come to baptize, or to ordain clergy, or to confirm the people. With the grace of the Lord, I did everything lovingly and gladly for your salvation.

All the while I used to give presents to the kings, besides the fees I paid to their sons who travel with me. Even so they laid hands on me and my companions, and on that day they eagerly wished to kill me; but my time had not yet come.

And everything they found with us they took away, and me they put in irons; and on the fourteenth day the Lord delivered me from their power, and our belongings were returned to us because of God and our dear friends whom we had seen before.

You know how much I paid to those who administered justice in all those districts to which I came frequently. I think I distributed among them not less than the price of fifteen men, so that you might enjoy me, and I might always enjoy you in God. I am not sorry for it---indeed it is not enough for me; I still spend and shall spend more. God has power to grant me afterwards that I myself may be spent for your souls.

Indeed, I call God to witness upon my soul that I lie not; neither, I hope, am I writing to you in order to make this an occasion of flattery or covetousness, nor because I look for honour from any of you. Sufficient is the honour that is not yet seen but is anticipated in the heart. Faithful is He that promised; He never lieth.

Saint Patrick   67

But I see myself exalted even in the present world beyond measure by the Lord, and I was not worthy nor such that He should grant me this. I know perfectly well, though not by my own judgement, that poverty and misfortune becomes me better than riches and pleasures.

For Christ the Lord, too, was poor for our sakes; and I, unhappy wretch that I am, have no wealth even if I wished for it. Daily I expect murder, fraud, or captivity, or whatever it may be; but I fear none of these things because of the promises of heaven. I have cast myself into the hands of God Almighty, who rules everywhere, as the prophet says: Cast thy thought upon God, and He shall sustain thee.

So, now I commend my soul to my faithful God, for whom I am an ambassador in all my wretchedness; but God accepteth no person, and chose me for this office---to be, although among His least, one of His ministers.

Hence let me render unto Him for all He has done to me. But what can I say or what can I promise to my Lord, as I can do nothing that He has not given me? May He search the hearts and deepest feelings; for greatly and exceedingly do I wish, and ready I was, that He should give me His chalice to drink, as He gave it also to the others who loved Him.

Wherefore may God never permit it to happen to me that I should lose His people which He purchased in the utmost parts of the world. I pray to God to give me perseverance and to deign that I be a faithful witness to Him to the end of my life for my God.

And if ever I have done any good for my God whom I love, I beg Him to grant me that I may shed my blood with those exiles and captives for His name, even though I should be denied a grave, or my body be woefully torn to pieces limb by limb by hounds or wild beasts, or the fowls of the air devour it. I am firmly convinced that if this should happen to me, I would have gained my soul together with my body, because on that day without doubt we shall rise in the brightness of the sun, that is, in the glory of Christ Jesus our Redeemer, as sons of the living God and joint heirs with Christ, to be made conformable to His image; for of Him, and by Him, and in Him we shall reign.

For this sun which we see rises daily for us because He commands so, but it will never reign, nor will its splendour last; what is more, those wretches who adore it will be miserably punished.

Not so we, who believe in, and worship, the true sun---Christ---who will never perish, nor will he who doeth His will; but he will abide for ever as Christ abideth for ever, who reigns with God the Father Almighty and the Holy Spirit before time, and now, and in all eternity. Amen.

Behold, again and again would I set forth the words of my confession. I testify in truth and in joy of heart before God and His holy angels that I never had any reason except the Gospel and its promises why I should ever return to the people from whom once before I barely escaped.

I pray those who believe and fear God, whosoever deigns to look at or receive this writing which Patrick, a sinner, unlearned, has composed in Ireland, that no one should ever say that it was my ignorance if I did or showed forth anything however small according to God's good pleasure; but let this be your conclusion and let it so be thought, that---as is the perfect truth---it was the gift of God.

This   is   my   confession   before   I   die.   [80]

LETTER TO COROTICUS

1. I, Patrick, a sinner, unlearned, resident in Ireland, declare myself to be a bishop. Most assuredly I believe that what I am I have received from God. And so I live among barbarians, a stranger and exile for the love of God. He is witness that this is so. Not that I wished my mouth to utter anything so hard and harsh; but I am forced by the zeal for God; and the truth of Christ has wrung it from me, out of love for my neighbors and sons for whom I gave up my country and parents and my life to the point of death. If I be worthy, I live for my God to teach the heathen, even though some may despise me.

2. With my own hand I have written and composed these words, to be given, delivered, and sent to the soldiers of Coroticus; I do not say, to my fellow citizens, or to fellow citizens of the holy Romans, but to fellow citizens of the demons, because of their evil works. Like our enemies, they live in death, allies of the Scots and the apostate Picts. Dripping with blood, they welter in the blood of innocent Christians, whom I have begotten into the number for God and confirmed in Christ!

3. The day after the newly baptized, anointed with chrism, in white garments (had been slain) - the fragrance was still on their foreheads when they were butchered and slaughtered with the sword by the above-mentioned people - I sent a letter with a holy presbyter whom I had taught from his childhood, clerics accompanying him, asking them to let us have some of the booty, and of the baptized they had made captives. They only jeered at them.

4. Hence I do not know what to lament more: those who have been slain, or those whom they have taken captive, or those whom the devil has mightily ensnared. Together with him they will be slaves in Hell in an eternal punishment; for who commits sin is a slave and will be called a son of the devil.

5. Wherefore let every God-fearing man know that they are enemies of me and of Christ my God, for whom I am an ambassador. Parricide! fratricide! ravening wolves that "eat the people of the Lord as they eat bread!" As is said, "the wicked, O Lord,

have destroyed Thy law," which but recently He had excellently and kindly planted in Ireland, and which had established itself by the grace of God.

6. I make no false claim. I share in the work of those whom He called and predestinated to preach the Gospel amidst grave persecutions unto the end of the earth, even if the enemy shows his jealousy through the tyranny of Coroticus, a man who has no respect for God nor for His priests whom He chose, giving them the highest, divine, and sublime power, that whom "they should bind upon earth should be bound also in Heaven."

7. Wherefore, then, I plead with you earnestly, ye holy and humble of heart, it is not permissible to court the favor of such people, nor to take food or drink with them, nor even to accept their alms, until they make reparation to God in hard-ships, through penance, with shedding of tears, and set free the baptized servants of God and handmaids of Christ, for whom He died and was crucified.

8. "The Most High disapproves the gifts of the wicked ... He that offers sacrifice of the goods of the poor, is as one that sacrifices the son in the presence of his lather. The riches, it is written, which he has gathered unjustly, shall be vomited up from his belly; the angel of death drags him away, by the fury of dragons he shall be tormented, the viper's tongue shall kill him, unquenchable fire devours him." And so - "woe to those who fill themselves with what is not their own;" or, "What does it profit a man that he gains the whole world, and suffers the loss of his own soul?

9. It would be too tedious to discuss and set forth everything in detail, to gather from the whole Law testimonies against such greed. Avarice is a deadly sin. "Thou shalt not covet thy neighbour' s goods." "Thou shalt not kill." A murderer cannot be with Christ. "Whosoever hates his brother is accounted a murderer." Or, "he that loves not his brother abides in death." How much more guilty is he that has stained his hands with blood of the sons of God whom He has of late purchased in the utmost part of the earth through the call of our littleness!

10. Did I come to Ireland without God, or according to the flesh? Who compelled me? I am bound by the Spirit not to see any of my kinsfolk. Is it of my own doing that I have holy mercy on the people who once took me captive and made away with the servants and maids of my father's house? I was freeborn according to the flesh. I am the son of a decurion. But I sold my noble rank I am neither ashamed nor sorry for the good of others. Thus I am a servant in Christ to a foreign nation for the unspeakable glory of life everlasting which is in Christ Jesus our Lord.

11. And if my own people do not know me, a prophet has no honor in his own country. Perhaps we are not of the same fold and have not one and the same God as father, as is written: "He that is not with me, is against me, and he that gathers not with me, scatters." It is not right that one destroys, another builds up. I seek not the things that are mine.

12. It is not my grace, but God who has given this solicitude into my heart, to be one of His hunters or fishers whom God once foretold would come in the last days.

13. I am hated. What shall I do, Lord? I am most despised. Look, Thy sheep around me are tom to pieces and driven away, and that by those robbers, by the orders of the hostile-minded Coroticus. Far from the love of God is a man who hands over Christians to the Picts and Scots. Ravening wolves have devoured the flock of the Lord, which in Ireland was indeed growing splendidly with the greatest care; and the sons and daughters of kings were monks and virgins of Christ - I cannot count their number. Wherefore, be not pleased with the wrong done to the just; even to hell it shall not please.

14. Who of the saints would not shudder to be merry with such persons or to enjoy a meal with them? They have filled their houses with the spoils of dead Christians, they live on plunder. They do not know, the wretches, that what they offer their friends and sons as food is deadly poison, just as Eve did not understand that it was death she gave to her husband. So are all that do evil: they work death as their eternal punishment.

15. This is the custom of the Roman Christians of Gaul [France]:

Saint Patrick

they send holy and able men to the Franks and other heathen with so many thousand solidi [gold coins] to ransom baptized captives. You prefer to kill and sell them to a foreign nation that has no knowledge of God. You betray the members of Christ as it were into a brothel. What hope have you in God, or anyone who thinks as you do, or converses with you in words of flattery? God will judge. For Scripture says: "Not only them that do evil are worthy to be condemned, but they also that consent to them."

16. I do not know why I should say or speak further about the departed ones of the sons of God, whom the sword has touched all too harshly. For Scripture says: "Weep with them that weep;" and again: "If one member be grieved, let all members grieve with it." Hence the Church mourns and laments her sons and daughters whom the sword has not yet slain, but who were removed and carried off to faraway lands, where sin abounds openly, grossly, impudently. There people who were freeborn have, been sold, Christians made slaves, and that, too, in the service of the abominable, wicked, and apostate Picts!

17. Therefore I shall raise my voice in sadness and grief- O you fair and beloved brethren and sons whom I have begotten in Christ, countless of number, what can I do you for? I am not worthy to come to the help of God or men. The wickedness of the wicked hath prevailed over us. We have been made, as it were, strangers. Perhaps they do not believe that we have received one and the same baptism, or have one and the same God as Father. For them it is a disgrace that we are Irish. Have ye not, as is written, one God? Have ye, every one of you, forsaken his neighbor?

18. Therefore I grieve for you, I grieve, my dearly beloved. But again, I rejoice within myself. I have not labored for nothing, and my journeying abroad has not been in vain. And if this horrible, unspeakable crime did happen - thanks be to God, you have left the world and have gone to Paradise as baptized faithful. I see you: you have begun to journey where night shall be no more, nor mourning, nor death; but you shall leap like calves loosened from their bonds, and you shall tread down the wicked, and they shall be ashes under your feet.

19. You then, will reign with the apostles, and prophets, and martyrs. You will take possession of an eternal kingdom, as He Himself testifies, saying: "They shall come from the east and from the west, and shall sit down with Abraham, and Isaac, and Jacob in the kingdom of heaven." "Without are dogs, and sorcerers,... and murderers; and liars and perjurers have their portion in the pool of everlasting fire." Not without reason does the Apostle say: "Where the just man shall scarcely be saved, where shall the sinner and ungodly transgressor of the law find himself?"

20. Where, then, will Coroticus with his criminals, rebels against Christ, where will they see themselves, they who distribute baptized women as prizes - for a miserable temporal kingdom, which will pass away in a moment? As a cloud or smoke that is dispersed by the wind, so shall the deceitful wicked perish at the presence of the Lord; but the just shall feast with great constancy with Christ, they shall judge nations, and rule over wicked kings for ever and ever. Amen.

21. I testify before God and His angels that it will be so as He indicated to my ignorance. It is not my words that I have set forth in Latin, but those of God and the apostles and prophets, who have never lied. "He that believes shall be saved; but he that believes not shall be condemned," God hath spoken.

22. I ask earnestly that whoever is a willing servant of God be a carrier of this letter, so that on no account it be suppressed or hidden by anyone, but rather be read before all the people, and in the presence of Coroticus himself. May God inspire them sometime to recover their senses for God, repenting, however late, their heinous deeds - murderers of the brethren of the Lord! - and to set free the baptized women whom they took captive, in order that they may deserve to live to God, and be made whole, here and in eternity! Be peace to the Father, and to the Son, and to the Holy Spirit. Amen.[81]

Excerpted notes on Letter To Coroticus:

Coroticus - Ceredig (other forms include Cerdic, Caradock, and Coroticus) was a common Welsh name which was popular with various dynasties (even in the non-Welsh kingdom of Wessex), there were several dark-age royals with that name. He is supposed to have been the king of Alcluid, a kingdom which would later be called Strathclyde. Alcluid was situated on the West Coast of Britain, several miles north of Cardigan, where another king lived with the same name; it was situated mostly between the Hadrianic and Antonine Walls -- in the semi-Romanized buffer zone between Barbarian Britain and Roman Britain.

Apostate Picts - Pictorum apostatarum. The pagan Scots of Argyleshire, descended from an Irish colony, who according to Dr. Todd, settled there in the third century, and the pagan Scots from Ireland, were long confederate with the Picts against the Roman power in Britain. The term apostate applies to the southern Picts, among whom Ninian had brought the gospel A.D. 412. The northern Picts were converted by the labors of Colum Cille A.D. 465.

PATRICK'S BREASTPLATE

(alternate translation)

1. I bind myself today to a strong virtue, an invocation of the Trinity.
I believe in a Threeness, with confession of an Oneness in the Creator of the Universe.

2. I bind myself today to the virtue of Christ's birth with his baptism,
to the virtue of his crucifixion with his burial,
to the virtue of his resurrection with his ascension,
to the virtue of his coming to the Judgment of Doom.

3. I bind myself today to the virtue of ranks of Cherubim,
in obedience of Angels,
[in service of Archangels]
in hope of resurrection for reward,
in prayers of Patriarchs,
in preaching of Apostles,
in faiths of Confessors,
in innocence of Holy Virgins,
in deeds of righteous men.

4. I bind myself today to the virtue of Heaven,
In light of Sun,
In brightness of Snow
In splendour of Fire,
In speed of Lightning,
In swiftness of Wind,
In depth of Sea,
In stability of Earth,
In compactness of Rock.

5. I bind myself today to God's Virtue to pilot me,
God's might to uphold me,

God's wisdom to guide me,
God's eye to look before me,
God's ear to hear me,
God's Word to speak to me,
God's hand to guard me,
God's way to lie before me,
God's shield to protect me,
God's host to secure me,
Against snares of demons,
Against seductions of vices,
Against lusts of nature,
Against every one who wishes ill to me,
Afar and a near,
Alone and in a multitude.

6. So have I invoked all these virtues between me,
[and these]
against every cruel, merciless power which may
come against my body an my soul
against incantations of false prophets,
against black laws of heathenry,
against false laws of heretics,
against craft of idolatry,
against spells of women and smiths and druids,
against every knowledge that defiles men's souls.

7. Christ to protect me today,
Against poison,
against burning,
against drowning,
against death-wound,
Until a multitude of rewards come to me!

8. Christ with me,
Christ before me,
Christ behind me,
Christ in me!
Christ below me,
Christ above me.
Christ at my right,
Christ at my left!

Christ in breadth,
Christ in length,
Christ in height!

9. Christ in the heart of everyone who thinks of me,
Christ in the mouth of everyone who speaks to me,
Christ in every eye that sees me,
Christ in every ear that hears me!

10. I bind myself today to a strong virtue,
An invocation of the Trinity.
I believe in a Threeness with confession of a Oneness,
in the Creator of [the Universe.]
Salvation is the Lord's,
Salvation is the Lord's,
Salvation is Christ's
May Thy salvation, O Lord, be always with us.[82]

Excerpted notes from: www.IrishChristian.com

The preface to this Hymn in the Book of Hymns states, in a very ancient dialect of Irish, that it is written "in the time of Loeghaire, son of Niall." Possibly not actually written by St. Patrick, but unquestionably reflects his faith. The translation and the notes are taken from "The Epistles & Hymn of Saint Patrick" by Thomas Olden, Dublin 1876. The notes have been edited by santing@irishchristian.com.

1. *Atomring* for ad-dom-ring; the verb *adring* is equivalent to *alligo*, "I bind to," with the personal pronoun dom "me." This expression seems to mean: "I connect myself with" or "I claim to have on my side."

3. *Inendgai noemingen* Some translate this line with "The purity of the Holy Virgin." However, the word is clearly plural. Neither St. Patrick nor Secundinus mention the "Holy Virgin."

4. The Irish deified the powers of nature, as appears from the case of King Laeghaire, (Leary,) who, being taken prisoner in battle, "swore by the Sun and Moon, the Water and the Air, Day and Night, Sea and Land, that he would never demand the Borumean tribute again;" but having broken his promise, "the Sun and Wind killed him." St. Patrick, as a Christian, claims to have them all on his site. "All things work together for good for them that love God." All things were his.

5. The bible portrays the demons as real beings, servants of Satan, fallen angels. They are active behind the scenes of the powers in the world and are ready to seduce the minds of sinful men. St. Patrick recognized the danger of these powers, and of their direct servants, the druids.

10. In the original, the last three lines are in Latin.

THE CODE OF ST. PATRIC

By Richard L. Federer, attorney
President, St. Louis Association of Realtors
(reprinted from the *St. Louis Post Dispatch*
Sunday, March 21, 1999, Section G)

Oh Begorrah! What is St. Patrick doing in the middle of a real estate column? And St. Paddy's day is gone and past at that!

Well, as if you hadn't heard enough about the Irish saint already, I thought you might want to know how he came to write the laws of Ireland down about the year 440.

It seems that when Patric, as he was known then, was around 33, he returned to Ireland from Auxerre, France, where he had been ordained. He was a missionary to Ireland and decided to try a new technique to gain Christians for the church.

Instead of converting individuals one by one, he first converted the King, a certain King O'Leary. The king saw to it that all of his subjects followed suit.

Patric and O'Leary hit it off quite well, and in 440 Patric persuaded the King to appoint a set of three kings, three historians and three priests to write down the common-law of Ireland in script.

You see, the common-law of Ireland was called the Brehon Law (from which we get Brian?") because the law was declared by the "brehons," the judges. It was an oral compilation of judicial decisions, mostly sung in couplets because it was too difficult to remember if merely spoken. It was handed down around the campfire from generation to generation. This may explain why Irish lawyers are such good singers!

At any event, the three sets of commissioners met at Tara, about 25 miles northwest of present day Dublin, and began their work. The work of the commission resulted in a 186-page book called the Senchus Mor, or Great Custom: The Customary or common-law.

80   *Saint Patrick*

There were five categories of land ownership. One type was the "ferann bord," or land of the table or the king's land. He held the land until his death then it went to his successor. This devolution was called the "tanistry."

Nobles held lands in fee and could divide their lands among their heirs during their lifetime but had no right to divide the lands to outsiders at death.

Tenants and lessees always paid their rent in kind: a cow, a days work or some other service. Leases ran typically for seven years and could be sublet.

Tribe or clan land was the fourth estate and any freeman (there were slaves) could occupy a part of it up to three years or upon his death. Then there was a "gavelkind" or redistribution.

Finally, there was a "common" tract of land where cattle were grazed and hunting was permitted.

Some of the laws were quite sound.

For instance, the judgement of Cormac states that if a sheep wanders into another's field and eats some of the crops thereon, the correct punishment in not the forfeiture of the sheep, but the forfeiture of the wool on the sheep. Both croppings of the grass and the wool are equal and both will grow back again.

Shouting at a pig and causing it to run into a person subjects the shouter to punitive as well as actual damages.

And that is the law, sure'n begorrah![83]

BIBLIOGRAPHY

Adamnan, *Life of Columba* (Adamnan was the ninth abbot of Iona, A.D. 688-692)

Bitel, Lisa. M., "Ascetic Superstars" (Christianity Today, Inc., 465 Gundersen Drive, Carol Stream, IL 60188, www.christianhistory.net, Issue 60, Vol. XVII, No. 4).

Bitel, Lisa, *Isle of the Saints* (Cornell University Press, 1990).

Burton, Louise Elaine, "Culture Clash – What Happened When Roman and Celtic Christianity Squared Off at the Synody of Whitby?" (Christianity Today, Inc., 465 Gundersen Drive, Carol Stream, IL 60188, www.christianhistory.net, Issue 60, Volume XVII, No. 4).

Cagney, Mary, "Patrick the Saint" (Christianity Today, Inc., 465 Gundersen Drive, Carol Stream, IL 60188, www.christianhistory.net, Issue 60, Volume XVII, No. 4).

Cahill, Thomas, "Ending Human Sacrifice" (Christianity Today, Inc., 465 Gundersen Drive, Carol Stream, IL 60188, www.christianhistory. net, Issue 60, Volume XVII, No. 4).

Cahill, Thomas, *How the Irish Saved Civilization – The Untold Story of Ireland's Heroic Role from the Fall of Rome to the Rise of Medieval Europe* (Doubleday, 1995).

Clancy, Thomas Owen, "Iona's Tough Dove" (Christianity Today, Inc., 465 Gundersen Drive, Carol Stream, IL 60188, www.christianhistory. net, Issue 60, Volume XVII, No. 4).

Clouse, Robert G., "Patrick," (Grand Rapids, MI: *Eerdmans' Handbook to the History of Christianity*, W.B Eerdmans' Publishing Co., 1988).

Cunliffe, Barry, *The Celtic World* (St. Martin's, 1990).

Davies, Oliver, and Bowie, Fiona, *Celtic Christian Spirituality: An Anthology of Medieval and Modern Sources* (SPCK, 1995). (Christianity Today, Inc., 465 Gundersen Drive, Carol Stream, IL 60188, www.christianhistory.net, Issue 60, Volume XVII, No. 4).

DePaor, Liam, *Saint Patrick's World* (University of Notre Dame, 1993).

Dowley, Tim, editor, *Eerdmans' Handbook to the History of Christianity* (Grand Rapids, MI: Wm. B. Eerdmans Publishing Co., 1977).

Dunlap, Ben, editor, *The Daily E-Pistle*, (The Catholic Community Forum, http://www.catholic-forum.com, http://www.ggdweb.com,

Liturgical Publications of St. Louis, Inc. http://www.liturgical.com 1-800-876-7000 or 314-394-7000).

Federer, Richard L., "The Code of St. Patric" (St. Louis Post Dispatch, March 21, 1999), section G.

Fremantle, Anne, et al., *Great Ages of Man--Age of Faith* (New York: Time-Life Books, 1965).

Galli, Mark, editor, "How the Irish Were Saved – The Culture and Faith of Celtic Christians" (Christianity Today, Inc., 465 Gundersen Drive, Carol Stream, IL 60188, www.christianhistory.net), Issue 60, Volume XVII, No. 4).

Hanson, R.P.C., *The Life and Writings of the Historical St. Patrick.*

Ironside, H.A., Litt. D. and Wimbish, John S., D.D., *The Real Saint Patrick* (Corona, NY: FBC Press, 105-01 37th Avenue, Corona, NY 11368, 718-457-5651, 1998).

Island Soldiers – video (Newbridge, Vision Video, 1997).

James, Simon, *The World of the Celts* (Thames and Hudson, 1993).

Linder, Robert D., "Columba – Missionary to the Scots," (John D. Woodbridge, *Great Leaders of the Christian Church*, Chicago, IL: Moody Press, 1988).

Mackey, James, P., editor, *An Introduction to Celtic Christianity.*

Markus, Gilbert, "Rooted in the Tradition" (Christianity Today, Inc., 465 Gundersen Drive, Carol Stream, IL 60188, www.christianhistory. net), Issue 60, Volume XVII, No. 4).

Mulhern, Kathy, "The Festive Abbess – Legendary Brigit" " (Christianity Today, Inc., 465 Gundersen Drive, Carol Stream, IL 60188, www.christianhistory.net), Issue 60, Volume XVII, No. 4).

O'Donohue, John, translator, *Confessions, Letter to Coroticus* (Doubleday, 1998).

Patrick, *Confessions; Letter to Coroticus; The Writings of Patrick; Book of Armagh.*

Pennick, Nigel, *Celtic Sacred Landscapes.*

Simons, Gerald, et al., *Great Ages of Man--Barbarian Europe* (New York: Time-Life Books, 1968).

Simpson, Ray, *Exploring Celtic Spirituality: Historic Roots for Our Future* (Hodder & Stoughton, 1995).

The Catholic Encyclopedia, Volume XI, (Copyright © 1911 by Robert Appleton Company, Online Edition Copyright © 1999 by Kevin Knight, Nihil Obstat, February 1, 1911. Remy Lafort, S.T.D., Censor, Imprimatur. +John Cardinal Farley, Archbishop of New

York)

The Ecole Initiative (www.evansville.edu/~ecoleweb/) The Christian Classics Ethereal Library (www.ccel.wheaton.edu).

The World Book Encyclopedia (Chicago, IL: Field Enterprises, Inc., 1957, volumes 13, 15).

Todd, Richard A., "The Fall of the Roman Empire" (*Eerdmans' Handbook to the History of Christianity,* Grand Rapids, MI: Wm. B. Eerdmans Publishing Co., 1977).

Tucker, Ruth A., *From Jerusalem to Irian Jaya* (Grand Rapids, MI: Academic Books, Zondervan Publishing House, 1983).

Unstead, R.J., *People in History-From Caractacus to Alfred* (London, England: A Carousel Book, Transworld Publishers, Ltd., 1975).

Webster's Family Encyclopedia (New York, NY: Ottenheimer Publishers, Inc., 1985), vol. 8, p. 1972; vol. 10, p. 2327).

Woodbridge, John D., *Great Leaders of the Christian Church* (Chicago, IL: Moody Press, 1988).

www.IrishChristian.com

ENDNOTES

1. Saint Patrick. *The Catholic Encyclopedia,* Volume XI, (Copyright © 1911 by Robert Appleton Company, Online Edition Copyright © 1999 by Kevin Knight Nihil Obstat, February 1, 1911. Remy Lafort, S.T.D., Censor, Imprimatur. +John Cardinal Farley, Archbishop of New York)

2. AD 385 (Saint Patrick FAQ http://www.Irishchristian.com/stpatrick/). A. D. 387 (*The World Book Encyclopedia* (Chicago, IL: Field Enterprises, Inc., 1957), vol. 13, p. 6142). AD 389 (Saint Patrick: History and Legend Roots-Web.com, Ancestry.com)http://www.rootsweb.com/~rwguide/notable/irish/stpatrick.html). A.D. 414 (Mary Cagney, "Patrick the Saint" (Christianity Today, Inc., 465 Gundersen Drive, Carol Stream, IL 60188, www.christianhistory.net), Issue 60, Volume XVII, No. 4, pp. 10-15). A.D. 415 (Liam de Paor, *Saint Patrick's World*, Notre Dame, 1993; Mark Galli, editor, "How the Irish Were Saved – The Culture and Faith of Celtic Christians" (Christianity Today, Inc., 465 Gundersen Drive, Carol Stream, IL 60188, www.christianhistory.net), Issue 60, Volume XVII, No. 4, 2).

3. H.A. Ironside, Litt. D. and John S. Wimbish, D.D., The Real Saint Patrick (Corona, NY: FBC Press, 105-01 37th Avenue, Corona, NY 11368, 718-457-5651, 1998), p. 7. http://www.newadvent.org/cathen/11554a.htm

4. Saint Patrick: History and Legend (RootsWeb.com, Ancestry.com) http://www.rootsweb.com/~rwguide/notable/irish/stpatrick.html

5. Saint Patrick: History and Legend (RootsWeb.com, Ancestry.com) http://www.rootsweb.com/~rwguide/notable/irish/stpatrick.html

6. R.J. Unstead, People in History-From Caractacus to Alfred (London, England: A Carousel Book, Transworld Publishers, Ltd., 1975), p. 33.

7. Annals of the Four Masters (Saint Patrick FAQ http://www.Irishchristian.com/stpatrick/) Some scholars suggest A.D. 492/493 - Mark Galli, editor, "How the Irish Were Saved – The Culture and Faith of Celtic Christians" (Christianity Today, Inc., 465 Gundersen Drive, Carol Stream, IL 60188, www.christianhistory.net), Issue 60, Volume XVII, No. 4.

8. Saint Patrick. *The Catholic Encyclopedia,* VolumeXI, (Copyright©1911, Robert Appleton Co., Online Edition Copyright©1999 by Kevin Knight Nihil Obstat, February 1, 1911. Remy Lafort, S.T.D., Censor, Imprimatur. +John Cardinal Farley, Archbishop of New York)

9. Mary Cagney, "Patrick the Saint" (Christianity Today, Inc., 465 Gundersen Drive, Carol Stream, IL 60188, www.christianhistory.net), Issue 60, Volume XVII, No. 4, p. 15.

10. Louise Elaine Burton, "Culture Clash – What Happened When Roman and Celtic Christianity Squared Off at the Synody of Whitby?" (Christianity Today, Inc., 465 Gundersen Drive, Carol Stream, IL 60188, www.christianhistory.net), Issue 60, Volume XVII, No. 4, pp. 38-40.

11. Patrick, *Confession*. Ludwig Bieler, translator, Christian Classics Ethereal Library www.ccel.org at Calvin College www.calvin.edu. (Also made available on the Internet by Patrick J. McGuinness, June 1997.) Other translations: John O'Donohue, translator, *Confessions, Letter to Coroticus* (Doubleday, 1998); R.P.C Hanson, *The Life and Writings of the Historical St. Patrick.* Actor Roger Nelson portrays Patrick of Ireland in a dramatic presentation of The Confession, and can be contacted at 1-818-794-3943, The Friends of St. Patrick, 1716 1/4 Sierra Bonita, Pasadena, CA 91104, courtesy of Michael K. Johnson, who posted The Confession of Saint Patrick on the Internet - johnsonm@redhat.com)

12. Patrick, *Confession*. Ludwig Bieler, translator, Christian Classics Ethereal Library www.ccel.org at Calvin College www.calvin.edu. (Also made available on the Internet by Patrick J. McGuinness, June 1997.) Other translations: John O'Donohue, translator, *Confessions, Letter to Coroticus* (Doubleday, 1998); R.P.C Hanson, *The Life and Writings of the Historical St. Patrick.* Actor Roger Nelson portrays Patrick of Ireland in a dramatic presentation of The Confession, and can be contacted at 1-818-794-3943, The Friends of St. Patrick, 1716 1/4 Sierra Bonita, Pasadena, CA 91104, courtesy of Michael K. Johnson, who posted The Confession of Saint Patrick on the Internet - johnsonm@redhat.com)

13. Salvian. Gerald Simons, et al., *Great Ages of Man--Barbarian Europe* (New York: Time-Life Books, 1968), p. 13. "For all the lurid Roman tales of their atrocities…[the barbarians] displayed…a good deal more fidelity to their wives."

14. Salvian. Gerald Simons, et al., *Great Ages of Man--Barbarian Europe* (New York: Time-Life Books, 1968), p. 15.

15. Gerald Simons, et al., *Great Ages of Man--Barbarian Europe* (New York: Time-Life Books, 1968), p. 20.

16. Gerald Simons, et al., *Great Ages of Man--Barbarian Europe* (New York: Time-Life Books, 1968), p. 18.

17. Salvian. Gerald Simons, et al., *Great Ages of Man--Barbarian Europe* (New York: Time-Life Books, 1968), p. 20.

18. Gerald Simons, et al., *Great Ages of Man--Barbarian Europe* (New York: Time-Life Books, 1968), p. 20.

19. Gerald Simons, et al., *Great Ages of Man--Barbarian Europe* (New York: Time-Life Books, 1968), p. 20.

20. Salvian. Gerald Simons, et al., *Great Ages of Man--Barbarian Europe* (New York: Time-Life Books, 1968), p. 39.

21. Richard A. Todd, "The Fall of the Roman Empire" (*Eerdmans' Handbook to the History of Christianity,* Grand Rapids, MI: Wm. B. Eerdmans Publishing Co., 1977), p. 184.

22. Mary Cagney, "Patrick the Saint" (Christianity Today, Inc., 465 Gundersen Drive, Carol Stream, IL 60188, www.christianhistory.net), Issue 60, Volume XVII, No. 4, p. 10.

23. Patrick, *Confession*. Ludwig Bieler, translator, Christian Classics Ethereal Library www.ccel.org at Calvin College www.calvin.edu. (Also made available on the Internet by Patrick J. McGuinness, June 1997.) Other translations: John O'Donohue, translator, *Confessions, Letter to Coroticus* (Doubleday, 1998); R.P.C Hanson, *The Life and Writings of the Historical St. Patrick.* Actor Roger Nelson portrays Patrick of Ireland in a dramatic presentation of The Confession, and can be contacted at 1-818-794-3943, The Friends of St. Patrick, 1716 1/4 Sierra Bonita, Pasadena, CA 91104, courtesy of Michael K. Johnson, who posted The Confession of Saint Patrick on the Internet - johnsonm@redhat.com)

24. Saint Patrick. *The Catholic Encyclopedia,* Vol. XI, (Copyright © 1911, Robert Appleton Co., Online Ed.Copyright © 1999, Kevin Knight Nihil Obstat, February 1, 1911. Remy Lafort, S.T.D., Censor, Imprimatur. +John Cardinal Farley, Archbishop of New York)

25. Mary Cagney, "Patrick the Saint" (Christianity Today, Inc., 465 Gundersen Drive, Carol Stream, IL 60188, www.christianhistory.net), Issue 60, Volume XVII, No. 4, pp. 11-12.

26. Thomas Cahill, "Ending Human Sacrifice" (Christianity Today, Inc., 465 Gundersen Drive, Carol Stream, IL 60188, www.christianhistory.net), Issue 60, Volume XVII, No. 4, pp. 16-17.

27. Patrick, *Confession*. Ludwig Bieler, translator, Christian Classics Ethereal Library www.ccel.org at Calvin College www.calvin.edu. (Also made available on the Internet by Patrick J. McGuinness, June 1997.) Other translations: John O'Donohue, translator, *Confessions, Letter to Coroticus* (Doubleday, 1998); R.P.C Hanson, *The Life and Writings of the Historical St. Patrick.* Actor Roger Nelson portrays Patrick of Ireland in a dramatic presentation of The Confession, and can be contacted at 1-818-794-3943, The Friends of St. Patrick, 1716 1/4 Sierra Bonita, Pasadena, CA 91104, courtesy of Michael K. Johnson, who posted The Confession of Saint Patrick on the Internet - johnsonm@redhat.com)

28.Saint Patrick. *The Catholic Encyclopedia,* Vol.XI, (Copyright©1911, Robert Appleton Co., Online Edition Copyright©1999 by Kevin Knight Nihil Obstat, February 1, 1911. Remy Lafort, S.T.D., Censor, Imprimatur. +John Cardinal Farley, Archbishop of New York)

29. Patrick, *Confession*. Ludwig Bieler, translator, Christian Classics Ethereal Library www.ccel.org at Calvin College www.calvin.edu. (Also made available on the Internet by Patrick J. McGuinness, June 1997.) Other translations: John O'Donohue, translator, *Confessions, Letter to Coroticus* (Doubleday, 1998); R.P.C Hanson, *The Life and Writings of the Historical St. Patrick.*)

30. Patrick, *Confession*. Ludwig Bieler, translator, Christian Classics Ethereal Library www.ccel.org at Calvin College www.calvin.edu. (Also made available on the Internet by Patrick J. McGuinness, June 1997.) Other translations: John O'Donohue, translator, *Confessions, Letter to Coroticus* (Doubleday, 1998); R.P.C Hanson, *The Life and Writings of the Historical St.*

Patrick. Actor Roger Nelson portrays Patrick of Ireland in a dramatic presentation of The Confession, and can be contacted at 1-818-794-3943, The Friends of St. Patrick, 1716 1/4 Sierra Bonita, Pasadena, CA 91104, courtesy of Michael K. Johnson, who posted The Confession of Saint Patrick on the Internet - johnsonm@redhat.com)

31. Mary Cagney, "Patrick the Saint" (Christianity Today, Inc., 465 Gundersen Drive, Carol Stream, IL 60188, www.christianhistory.net), Issue 60, Volume XVII, No. 4, p. 12.

32. Patrick, *Confession.* Ludwig Bieler, translator, Christian Classics Ethereal Library www.ccel.org at Calvin College www.calvin.edu. (Also made available on the Internet by Patrick J. McGuinness, June 1997.) Other translations: John O'Donohue, translator, *Confessions, Letter to Coroticus* (Doubleday, 1998); R.P.C Hanson, *The Life and Writings of the Historical St. Patrick.* Actor Roger Nelson portrays Patrick of Ireland in a dramatic presentation of The Confession, and can be contacted at 1-818-794-3943, The Friends of St. Patrick, 1716 1/4 Sierra Bonita, Pasadena, CA 91104, courtesy of Michael K. Johnson, who posted The Confession of Saint Patrick on the Internet - johnsonm@redhat.com)

33. R.J. Unstead, People in History-From Caractacus to Alfred (London, England: A Carousel Book, Transworld Publishers, Ltd., 1975), p. 35.

34 Mary Cagney, "Patrick the Saint" (Christianity Today, Inc., 465 Gundersen Drive, Carol Stream, IL 60188, www.christianhistory.net), Issue 60, Volume XVII, No. 4, p. 12.

35. Patrick, *Confession.* Ludwig Bieler, translator, Christian Classics Ethereal Library www.ccel.org at Calvin College www.calvin.edu. (Also made available on the Internet by Patrick J. McGuinness, June 1997.) Other translations: John O'Donohue, translator, *Confessions, Letter to Coroticus* (Doubleday, 1998); R.P.C Hanson, *The Life and Writings of the Historical St. Patrick.* Actor Roger Nelson portrays Patrick of Ireland in a dramatic presentation of The Confession, and can be contacted at 1-818-794-3943, The Friends of St. Patrick, 1716 1/4 Sierra Bonita, Pasadena, CA 91104, courtesy of Michael K. Johnson, who posted The Confession of Saint Patrick on the Internet - johnsonm@redhat.com)

36. Patrick, *Confession.* Ludwig Bieler, translator, Christian Classics Ethereal Library www.ccel.org at Calvin College www.calvin.edu. (Also made available on the Internet by Patrick J. McGuinness, June 1997.) Other translations: John O'Donohue, translator, *Confessions, Letter to Coroticus* (Doubleday, 1998); R.P.C Hanson, *The Life and Writings of the Historical St. Patrick.* Actor Roger Nelson portrays Patrick of Ireland in a dramatic presentation of The Confession, and can be contacted at 1-818-794-3943, The Friends of St. Patrick, 1716 1/4 Sierra Bonita, Pasadena, CA 91104, courtesy of Michael K. Johnson, who posted The Confession of Saint Patrick on the Internet - johnsonm@redhat.com)

37. Patrick, *Confession.* Ludwig Bieler, translator, Christian Classics Ethereal Library www.ccel.org at Calvin College www.calvin.edu. (Also

made available on the Internet by Patrick J. McGuinness, June 1997.) Other translations: John O'Donohue, translator, *Confessions, Letter to Coroticus* (Doubleday, 1998); R.P.C Hanson, *The Life and Writings of the Historical St. Patrick.* Actor Roger Nelson portrays Patrick of Ireland in a dramatic presentation of The Confession, and can be contacted at 1-818-794-3943, The Friends of St. Patrick, 1716 1/4 Sierra Bonita, Pasadena, CA 91104, courtesy of Michael K. Johnson, who posted The Confession of Saint Patrick on the Internet - johnsonm@redhat.com)

38. Patrick, *Confession.* Ludwig Bieler, translator, Christian Classics Ethereal Library www.ccel.org at Calvin College www.calvin.edu. (Also made available on the Internet by Patrick J. McGuinness, June 1997.) Other translations: John O'Donohue, translator, *Confessions, Letter to Coroticus* (Doubleday, 1998); R.P.C Hanson, *The Life and Writings of the Historical St. Patrick.* Actor Roger Nelson portrays Patrick of Ireland in a dramatic presentation of The Confession, and can be contacted at 1-818-794-3943, The Friends of St. Patrick, 1716 1/4 Sierra Bonita, Pasadena, CA 91104, courtesy of Michael K. Johnson, who posted The Confession of Saint Patrick on the Internet - johnsonm@redhat.com)

39. Patrick, *Confession.* Ludwig Bieler, translator, Christian Classics Ethereal Library www.ccel.org at Calvin College www.calvin.edu. (Also made available on the Internet by Patrick J. McGuinness, June 1997.) Other translations: John O'Donohue, translator, *Confessions, Letter to Coroticus* (Doubleday, 1998); R.P.C Hanson, *The Life and Writings of the Historical St. Patrick.* Actor Roger Nelson portrays Patrick of Ireland in a dramatic presentation of The Confession, and can be contacted at 1-818-794-3943, The Friends of St. Patrick, 1716 1/4 Sierra Bonita, Pasadena, CA 91104, courtesy of Michael K. Johnson, who posted The Confession of Saint Patrick on the Internet - johnsonm@redhat.com)

40. Mary Cagney, "Patrick the Saint" (Christianity Today, Inc., 465 Gundersen Drive, Carol Stream, IL 60188, www.christianhistory.net), Issue 60, Volume XVII, No. 4, p. 12.

41. www.worldbookonline.com William J. Courtenay, "Patrick, Saint," *World Book Online Americas Edition*, http://www.aolsvc.worldbook.aol. com/wbol/wbPage/na/ar/co/417760, April 4, 2002. William J. Courtenay, Ph.D., Professor of Medieval History, University of Wisconsin, Madison.

42. Patrick, *Confession.* Ludwig Bieler, translator, Christian Classics Ethereal Library www.ccel.org at Calvin College www.calvin.edu. (Also made available on the Internet by Patrick J. McGuinness, June 1997.) Other translations: John O'Donohue, translator, *Confessions, Letter to Coroticus* (Doubleday, 1998); R.P.C Hanson, *The Life and Writings of the Historical St. Patrick.* Actor Roger Nelson portrays Patrick of Ireland in a dramatic presentation of The Confession, and can be contacted at 1-818-794-3943, The Friends of St. Patrick, 1716 1/4 Sierra Bonita, Pasadena, CA 91104, courtesy of Michael K. Johnson, who posted The Confession of Saint Patrick on the Internet - johnsonm@redhat.com)

43. Saint Patrick. *The Catholic Encyclopedia,*Vol.XI, (Copyright©1911, Robert Appleton Co., Online Ed. Copyright©1999,Kevin Knight Nihil Obstat, February 1, 1911. Remy Lafort, S.T.D., Censor, Imprimatur. +John Cardinal Farley, Archbishop of New York)

44. Mary Cagney, "Patrick the Saint" (Christianity Today, Inc., 465 Gundersen Drive, Carol Stream, IL 60188, www.christianhistory.net), Issue 60, Volume XVII, No. 4, p. 12.

45. Mary Cagney, "Patrick the Saint" (Christianity Today, Inc., 465 Gundersen Drive, Carol Stream, IL 60188, www.christianhistory.net), Issue 60, Volume XVII, No. 4, p. 12.

46. Saint Patrick. *The Catholic Encyclopedia,*Vol.XI, (Copyright©1911, Robert Appleton Co., Online Edition Copyright©1999, Kevin Knight Nihil Obstat, February 1, 1911. Remy Lafort, S.T.D., Censor, Imprimatur. +John Cardinal Farley, Archbishop of New York)

47. R.J. Unstead, *People in History-From Caractacus to Alfred* (London, England: A Carousel Book, Transworld Publishers, Ltd., 1975), p. 36.

48. Saint Patrick. Another story is that Milchu, upon hearing of Patrick's return to Ireland, set his mansion aflame and threw himself in, as "his pride could not endure the thought of being vanquished by a former slave." *The Catholic Encyclopedia,* Vol.XI, (Copyright©1911, Robert Appleton Co., Online Edition Copyright © 1999, Kevin Knight Nihil Obstat, February 1, 1911. Remy Lafort, S.T.D., Censor, Imprimatur. +John Cardinal Farley, Archbishop of New York)

49. R.J. Unstead, *People in History-From Caractacus to Alfred* (London, England: A Carousel Book, Transworld Publishers, Ltd., 1975), p. 36.

50. Encyclopedia Britannica (Copyright 1946), Volume 17, page 383. H. A. Ironside, Litt. D. and John S. Wimbish, D.D., *The Real Saint Patrick* (Corona, NY: FBC Press, 105-01 37ᵗʰ Avenue, Corona, NY 11368, 718-457-5651, 1998), p. 26.

51. H.A. Ironside, Litt. D. and John S. Wimbish, D.D., *The Real Saint Patrick* (Corona, NY: FBC Press, 105-01 37ᵗʰ Avenue, Corona, NY 11368, 718-457-5651, 1998), p. 26.

52. Mary Cagney, "Patrick the Saint" (Christianity Today, Inc., 465 Gundersen Drive, Carol Stream, IL 60188, www.christianhistory.net), Issue 60, Volume XVII, No. 4, p. 12.

53. Saint Patrick. *The Catholic Encyclopedia,*Vol.XI, (Copyright©1911, Robert Appleton Co., Online Edition Copyright©1999, Kevin Knight Nihil Obstat, February 1, 1911. Remy Lafort, S.T.D., Censor, Imprimatur. +John Cardinal Farley, Archbishop of New York)

54. Patrick, *Confession.* Ludwig Bieler, translator, Christian Classics Ethereal Library www.ccel.org at Calvin College www.calvin.edu. (Also made available on the Internet by Patrick J. McGuinness, June 1997.) Other translations: John O'Donohue, translator, *Confessions, Letter to Coroticus* (Doubleday, 1998); R.P.C Hanson, *The Life and Writings of the Historical St. Patrick.* Actor Roger Nelson portrays Patrick of Ireland in a

dramatic presentation of The Confession, and can be contacted at 1-818-794-3943, The Friends of St. Patrick, 1716 1/4 Sierra Bonita, Pasadena, CA 91104, courtesy of Michael K. Johnson, who posted The Confession of Saint Patrick on the Internet - johnsonm@redhat.com)

55. Patrick, *Confession.* Ludwig Bieler, translator, Christian Classics Ethereal Library www.ccel.org at Calvin College www.calvin.edu. (Also made available on the Internet by Patrick J. McGuinness, June 1997.) Other translations: John O'Donohue, translator, *Confessions, Letter to Coroticus* (Doubleday, 1998); R.P.C Hanson, *The Life and Writings of the Historical St. Patrick.* Actor Roger Nelson portrays Patrick of Ireland in a dramatic presentation of The Confession, and can be contacted at 1-818-794-3943, The Friends of St. Patrick, 1716 1/4 Sierra Bonita, Pasadena, CA 91104, courtesy of Michael K. Johnson, who posted The Confession of Saint Patrick on the Internet - johnsonm@redhat.com)

56. Thomas Cahill, "Ending Human Sacrifice" (Christianity Today, Inc., 465 Gundersen Drive, Carol Stream, IL 60188, www.christianhistory.net), Issue 60, Volume XVII, No. 4, p. 18.

57. Mary Cagney, "Patrick the Saint" (Christianity Today, Inc., 465 Gundersen Drive, Carol Stream, IL 60188, www.christianhistory.net), Issue 60, Volume XVII, No. 4, p. 14.

58. Mary Cagney, "Patrick the Saint" (Christianity Today, Inc., 465 Gundersen Drive, Carol Stream, IL 60188, www.christianhistory.net), Issue 60, Volume XVII, No. 4, p. 14.

59. Mary Cagney, "Patrick the Saint" (Christianity Today, Inc., 465 Gundersen Drive, Carol Stream, IL 60188, www.christianhistory.net), Issue 60, Volume XVII, No. 4, p. 14.

60. Patrick, *Confession.* Ludwig Bieler, translator, Christian Classics Ethereal Library www.ccel.org at Calvin College www.calvin.edu. (Also made available on the Internet by Patrick J. McGuinness, June 1997.) Other translations: John O'Donohue, translator, *Confessions, Letter to Coroticus* (Doubleday, 1998); R.P.C Hanson, *The Life and Writings of the Historical St. Patrick.* Actor Roger Nelson portrays Patrick of Ireland in a dramatic presentation of The Confession, and can be contacted at 1-818-794-3943, The Friends of St. Patrick, 1716 1/4 Sierra Bonita, Pasadena, CA 91104, courtesy of Michael K. Johnson, who posted The Confession of Saint Patrick on the Internet - johnsonm@redhat.com)

61. Patrick, Letter to Coroticus. Translated by Ludwig Bieler, scanned in and made available electronically by Patrick J. McGuinness, with thanks, June 1997.

62. *The World Book Encyclopedia* (Chicago, IL: Field Enterprises, Inc., 1957), vol. 15, p. 7395.

63. Patrick, *Confession.* Ludwig Bieler, translator, Christian Classics Ethereal Library www.ccel.org at Calvin College www.calvin.edu. (Also made available on the Internet by Patrick J. McGuinness, June 1997.) Other translations: John O'Donohue, translator, *Confessions, Letter to Coroti-*

cus (Doubleday, 1998); R.P.C Hanson, *The Life and Writings of the Historical St. Patrick.* Actor Roger Nelson portrays Patrick of Ireland in a dramatic presentation of The Confession, and can be contacted at 1-818-794-3943, The Friends of St. Patrick, 1716 1/4 Sierra Bonita, Pasadena, CA 91104, courtesy of Michael K. Johnson, who posted The Confession of Saint Patrick on the Internet - johnsonm@redhat.com)

64. Patrick, *Confession.* Ludwig Bieler, translator, Christian Classics Ethereal Library www.ccel.org at Calvin College www.calvin.edu. (Also made available on the Internet by Patrick J. McGuinness, June 1997.) Other translations: John O'Donohue, translator, *Confessions, Letter to Coroticus* (Doubleday, 1998); R.P.C Hanson, *The Life and Writings of the Historical St. Patrick.*)

65. Mary Cagney, "Patrick the Saint" (Christianity Today, Inc., 465 Gundersen Drive, Carol Stream, IL 60188, www.christianhistory.net), Issue 60, Volume XVII, No. 4, pp. 14.-15

66. Patrick, *Confession.* Ludwig Bieler, translator, Christian Classics Ethereal Library www.ccel.org at Calvin College www.calvin.edu. (Also made available on the Internet by Patrick J. McGuinness, June 1997.) Other translations: John O'Donohue, translator, *Confessions, Letter to Coroticus* (Doubleday, 1998); R.P.C Hanson, *The Life and Writings of the Historical St. Patrick.*)

67. Patrick, *Confession.* Ludwig Bieler, translator, Christian Classics Ethereal Library www.ccel.org at Calvin College www.calvin.edu. (Also made available on the Internet by Patrick J. McGuinness, June 1997.) Other translations: John O'Donohue, translator, *Confessions, Letter to Coroticus* (Doubleday, 1998); R.P.C Hanson, *The Life and Writings of the Historical St. Patrick.*)

68. Patrick, *Confession.* Ludwig Bieler, translator, Christian Classics Ethereal Library www.ccel.org at Calvin College www.calvin.edu. (Also made available on the Internet by Patrick J. McGuinness, June 1997.) Other translations: John O'Donohue, translator, *Confessions, Letter to Coroticus* (Doubleday, 1998); R.P.C Hanson, *The Life and Writings of the Historical St. Patrick.*)

69. *The World Book Encyclopedia* (Chicago, IL: Field Enterprises, Inc., 1957), vol. 13, p. 6142.

70. Synod of Whitby. Herbert Thurston, transcribed by Paul Knutsen, *The Catholic Encyclopedia,* VolumeXI, (Copyright©1911 by Robert Appleton Company, Online Edition Copyright©1999 by Kevin Knight Nihil Obstat, February 1, 1911. Remy Lafort, S.T.D., Censor, Imprimatur. +John Cardinal Farley, Archbishop of New York)

71. Robert D. Linder, "Columba – Missionary to the Scots," contained in John D. Woodbridge's *Great Leaders of the Christian Church* (Chicago, IL: Moody Press, 1988), p. 100.

72. Tucker, Ruth A., *From Jerusalem to Irian Jaya* (Grand Rapids, MI: Academic Books, Zondervan Publishing House, 1983), pp. 38 - 40.

73. Thomas Owen Clancy, "Iona's Tough Dove" (Christianity Today, Inc., 465 Gundersen Drive, Carol Stream, IL 60188, www.christianhistory.net), Issue 60, Volume XVII, No. 4, pp. 27-29.

74. Ted Olson, "Missionary Inflexible – The handsome and hot-headed Columbanus was one of Western Europe's most successful evangelists ever" (Markus, Gilbert, "Rooted in the Tradition" (Christianity Today, Inc., 465 Gundersen Drive, Carol Stream, IL 60188, www.christianhistory.net), Issue 60, Volume XVII, No. 4, pp. 35-36

75. Patrick, *Confession*. Ludwig Bieler, translator, Christian Classics Ethereal Library www.ccel.org at Calvin College www.calvin.edu. (Also made available on the Internet by Patrick J. McGuinness, June 1997.) Other translations: John O'Donohue, translator, *Confessions, Letter to Coroticus* (Doubleday, 1998); R.P.C Hanson, *The Life and Writings of the Historical St. Patrick.*).

76. Mary Cagney, "Patrick the Saint" (Christianity Today, Inc., 465 Gundersen Drive, Carol Stream, IL 60188, www.christianhistory.net), Issue 60, Volume XVII, No. 4, p. 14.

77. *The World Book Encyclopedia* (Chicago, IL: Field Enterprises, Inc., 1957), vol. 13, p. 6142; vol. 13, p. 6142.

78. Patrick, *Confession*. Ludwig Bieler, translator, Christian Classics Ethereal Library www.ccel.org at Calvin College www.calvin.edu. (Also made available on the Internet by Patrick J. McGuinness, June 1997.) Other translations: John O'Donohue, translator, *Confessions, Letter to Coroticus* (Doubleday, 1998); R.P.C Hanson, *The Life and Writings of the Historical St. Patrick.*)

79. Patrick's Breastplate, (Also known as the Shield of Patrick, and the Deer's Cry), paraphrased by Mrs. Cecil Frances Alexander, Dowley, Tim, editor, Eerdmans' Handbook to the History of Christianity (Grand Rapids, MI: Wm. B. Eerdmans Publishing Co., 1977), p. 212.

80. Patrick, *Confession*. Ludwig Bieler, translator, Christian Classics Ethereal Library www.ccel.org at Calvin College www.calvin.edu. (Also made available on the Internet by Patrick J. McGuinness, June 1997.) Other translations: John O'Donohue, translator, *Confessions, Letter to Coroticus* (Doubleday, 1998); R.P.C Hanson, *The Life and Writings of the Historical St. Patrick.*).

81. Patrick, Letter to Coroticus. Translated by Ludwig Bieler, scanned in and made available electronically by Patrick J. McGuinness, with thanks, June 1997.

82. Patrick's Breastplate (www.IrishChristian.com).

83. Richard L. Federer, "The Code of Patric" (St. Louis Post Dispatch, Section G, March 21, 1999).

Saint Patrick

Other Amerisearch, Inc., publications:

**AMERICA'S GOD AND COUNTRY
ENCYCLOPEDIA OF QUOTATIONS**
By William J. Federer

$29.99 Hardcover (ISBN 1-880563-09-6)
$19.99 Paperback (ISBN 1-880563-05-3)

Best-selling resource of profound quotes highlighting America's noble heritage. Over 200,000 in print! 845 pages of quotations from Presidents, Statesmen, Acts of Congress, Supreme Court Decisions, State Constitutions, Colonial Charters, Scientists, Explorers, Pioneers, Business Leaders, Military Leaders... on topics such as: character, virtue, law, freedom, courage, liberty, Providence, God, Deity, religion, morality, faith...

Easy to use, alphabetically arranged, fully footnoted, with subject and entry index. A favorite of national leaders, politicians, teachers, etc. No American library is complete without this classic! (845 pages)

AMERICAN QUOTATIONS
By William J. Federer
$49.99 (ISBN 0-9653557-1-3)
The most comprehensive CD ROM resource on America's noble heritage. 1000's of quotations from famous men, women, historical documents, court decisions, memoirs, colonial charters, scientists, politicians, military leaders, explorers, pioneers...

*Easy-to-use   *Search by word, phrase, entry
*Quickly cut & paste   *Chronologically arranged
*Fully footnoted   *Highlighted pop-up dictionary

Contains *America's God and Country Encyclopedia of Quotations* plus thousands of additional quotes, *Noah Webster's original 1828 Dictionary, King James Bible, Strong's Greek & Hebrew Definitions, Nave's Topical Index*. Ideal for speeches, reports, letters-to-the-editor, etc. A great gift for teachers, journalists, politicians, students, graduation presents! (uses MS Windows)

CPSIA information can be obtained
at www.ICGtesting.com
Printed in the USA
LVHW08s1521170718
584080LV00001B/33/P